THE WHOLE HERB

THE WHOLE HERB

FOR COOKING, CRAFTS, GARDENING, HEALTH, AND OTHER JOYS OF LIFE

BARBARA PLEASANT

SQUAREONE
PUBLISHERS

The information contained in this book regarding the therapeutic use of herbs is based upon the research of the author. It is not intended as a substitute for consulting with your physician or other health care provider. The publisher and author are not responsible for any adverse effects or consequences resulting from the use of any of the suggestions or preparations discussed in this book. All matters pertaining to your physical health should be supervised by a health care professional. It is a sign of wisdom, not cowardice, to seek a second or third opinion.

COVER DESIGNER: Phaedra Mastrocola • COVER PHOTO: Getty Images, Inc.
TEXT ILLUSTRATOR: Vicki Renoux • TYPESETTER: Gary A. Rosenberg
EDITOR: Carol Rosenberg • IN-HOUSE EDITOR: Marie Caratozzolo
PHOTOGRAPH ON PAGE 19: © The Bach Centre, Mount Vernon, Sotwell, England.

Square One Publishers
115 Herricks Road • Garden City Park, NY 11040
(516) 535-2010 • (877) 900-BOOK • www.squareonepublishers.com

Library of Congress Cataloging-in-Publication Data
Pleasant, Barbara.
    The whole herb : for cooking, crafts, gardening, health,
and other joys of life / Barbara Pleasant.
    p. cm.
    ISBN 0-7570-0080-0 (pbk.)
    1. Herbs. 2. Herb gardening. 3. Cookery (Herbs)
4. Herbs—Utilization. 5. Handicraft. I. Title.
SB351.H5 P64   2004
635'.7—dc22   2003026306

635   H
PLE   11-6-08

Printed in the United States of America

10 9 8 7 6 5 4 3 2 1

Contents

Introduction

THDRAWN

 Welcome to the wonderful world of herbs. If you are reading this book, chances are herbs have already caught your interest, and you are curious about these intriguing plants. Great! The purpose of this book is to give you a solid sampling of everything herbs have to offer—in the medicine cabinet, in the kitchen, on the craft table, or in your garden.

As you will discover in the following pages, herbs are among the most fascinating and useful plants on earth. Their value to humankind has proved to be timeless. In the age of modern science, new knowledge about herbs is constantly emerging, and up-to-date information is an important focus of this book. The historical value of herbs remains significant, but it is considered alongside sound, practical insights into their uses gleaned from the world of science.

Part One of this book is designed to help you understand herbs, how they have earned their place in today's world, and the many uses you will find for them in your own life. In Chapter 1, we will define herbs, review their facinating history, and sort through their many uses, past and present. Much herbal lore came to us from Europe, but Native American medicines and rituals have further enriched the history of herbs.

Chapter 2 explores how herbs are used to make people feel better, whether their effects are enhancing well-being or curing illness. We will follow the story of healing herbs from its beginning, which can be traced back at least 3,500 years, and then look at how modern medicinal herbs are processed, packaged, and sold. If you grow your own medicinal herbs, methods for transforming them into teas or tinctures that can be stored until they are needed also get their turn in this chapter. And, since few things are more important than your health, safety questions that pertain to medicinal herbs will be given careful coverage, too.

If you want to be a better cook, Chapter 3 explains how to choose, use, and store fine culinary herbs, as well as how to combine them in classic dishes. You will learn which herbs go together and which ones do not, and you will be offered a buffet of great ideas for using culinary herbs. From how to make herbal vinegars to freezing sprigs of mint in cubes of cranberry juice, cooking with herbs is easy. For meat lovers, there are recipes for dry rubs—the secret behind herb-encrusted anything.

When your hands itch for a creative project with herbs, Chapter 4 will get you going. Along with techniques for making long-lasting potpourri and beautiful herbal wreaths, this is where you'll learn the symbolic meanings of different herbs, and discover how they have inspired the thoughts and feelings of people for many generations. This is also the place to find information on using essential oils in massage and other forms of aromatherapy, and how to use herbs to turn a bath into a mood-altering experience.

Chapter 5 takes you to the place where an herb-inspired heart naturally gravitates, the garden. Many herbs are very easy to grow, and some are so beautiful that you may hesitate to pick them. If you're short on time and space, you may still want to grow a "container bouquet" of culinary herbs in the summer, or keep an aloe or bay plant indoors year-round. For herb gardeners with greater aspirations, there are instructions for rooting stem cuttings and other methods of plant propagation.

To bring together as much information as possible on individual herbs, Part Two provides comprehensive coverage of fifty-five essential herbs and shows how they are used for medicinal, culinary, aromatic, and ornamental purposes. As you discover new herbs, Part Two is the place to look for concise information about them.

Whether you want to use herbs to create better health, better meals, unforgettable fragrances, or a beautiful garden to behold when you look out your back door, this book is here to help. One thing you won't find in this book is herbal hype, because herbs don't need exaggerated claims. Approached with a curious mind and taken up by caring hands, herbs are good enough just as they are. This is something that you will discover each time you use herbs. Herbs are really very basic plants that have been serving people for a very long time. Expect to be pleasantly surprised with how comfortable it feels to include them in your life.

PART ONE

AllAbout**Herbs**

CHAPTER 1

Herbs,Health, and**Happiness**

 What are herbs, and how can you use them? I always think of herbs as Nature's treasure plants because they are such rich stores of goodness. Herbs are incredibly versatile. They can delight your senses, improve your diet, boost your immune system, help you rest, sharpen your mind, and make you smell nice, too.

As you learn more about herbs, you'll be amazed at the many ways they can enrich your life. Perhaps you will find one to help cure a nagging health problem you're experiencing, or maybe you'll discover the fun of arranging herbs and flowers into beautiful wreaths, swags, or tiny hand-sized bouquets called tussie-mussies, which were the rage among Victorian-era English ladies. If you want to grow herbs, why wait? You can easily cultivate a small collection of flavorful culinary herbs in pots, or fill a corner of your yard with varieties that are most valued for their eye-appeal and/or wonderful aroma.

In this chapter, we will present the many definitions of herbs (as you'll see, they mean different things to different people), sort through their many available forms in the marketplace, and take a look at their fascinating history. Then we'll present some of the many ways you can use herbs to enhance and improve you life.

DEFINING HERBS

Because herbs are such versatile plants, arriving at a firm definition can be tricky. For example, botanists, cooks, herbal healers, and massage therapists use very different definitions for herbs:

🌿 Botanists (plant scientists) often use the word "herb" to describe plants without woody stems that grow through spring, summer, and autumn, and then die back to the ground in winter. By this definition, petunias and pansies are herbs, as are crabgrass and lettuce.

🌿 To cooks, herbs are plants that are used to add interesting flavors to foods. Typically, herbs are the stems, leaves, and flowers of a plant, while spices are derived from seeds.

🌿 To herbalists or herbal healers, numerous everyday foods such as pineapple, mushrooms, and cooked greens fall into the category of herbs, along with plants that are widely recognized for their medicinal properties such as aloe and feverfew.

🌿 To a massage therapist, herbs are plants valued primarily for their aromas, especially when their relaxing, stimulating, or soothing effects are combined with skilled human touch. Tree barks and oils make their way into this definition of herbs, as do fragrances derived from fruits.

These definitions have one thing in common—herbs are plants that have special talents for enhancing the quality of our lives. It is this simplified definition that I will use in this book.

Not surprisingly, herbs are perhaps the most likely of all plants to give rise to a certain passion among people who get to know them. Once you make friends with herbs, you'll want to learn more about them. And there are always new things to discover about these remarkable plants.

THE HERBAL MARKETPLACE

A century ago, herbs were available in only two forms. They were either live plants, being tended in a garden, or precious caches of preserved herbs, which were carefully stored for off-season use. Today, herbs remain prime candidates for any garden, but they are also widely available as packaged products. Supermarkets sell dried culinary herbs on the spice shelf, as well as fresh varieties in the produce section. Alongside regular tea, you will find herbal teas, including some that have medicinal or nutritional value. Craft stores offer packages of dried herbs to use in making potpourri, as well as decorative long-stemmed herbs that have been dried in bunches. In summer, freshly cut culinary and craft herbs are available at many farmers' markets; the rest of the year, they can be purchased directly from farmers who sell them on the Internet or by mail order. If you want to grow your own herbs, you can order plants and seeds this way, too. The Resources section, beginning on page 229, provides numerous mail-order and Internet sources for seeds, plants, dried herbs, and medicinal herbal products.

Like many household necessities, herbs and herbal products were once commonly sold in outdoor markets.

A visit to any health food store, herb shop, or even a large drugstore or supermarket will reveal a mind-boggling selection of health-enhancing herbs sold as tablets, capsules, powders, teas, liquid extracts, and tonics that are taken internally. In addition, there are topical lotions, creams, and even toothpastes that contain healing herbs.

How do you know which ones to choose? Chapter 2 will steer you in the right direction. It also provides instructions for some herbal remedies you can make yourself. But if you still have questions, ask them! At stores that specialize in natural health products, employees are accustomed to questions and to helping customers find products that best suit their needs. The same is true of many pharmacies.

You may want to experiment with different forms of a certain herb in search of favorites. For example, if you are pleased with the effectiveness of a tea or a tincture but don't like its taste, you can always switch to a capsule. There are also special herbal products for children, developed specifically for their kid-sized bodies and finicky palates. These herbal remedies usually take the form of sweet-tasting syrups.

Indeed, there has never been a better time to discover the flavors, beauty, and health benefits of herbs. Some herbs that were once obscure, such as ginkgo, are now sold alongside vitamins. Today's widespread availability of herbs—the latest chapter in its history—is a neat story in itself, and is discussed briefly below.

A BRIEF HISTORY OF HERBS

Imagine a world in which you ate the same foods day after day; a place where people rarely bathed, bathrooms and running water were nonexistent, and sickness often led to death. Further imagine that in this world food poisoning and dental problems were everyday occurrences, and few people lived past the age of forty.

Such was the human condition for many thousands of years. And yet, when surveying the history of mankind and noting the common threads that helped people improve the quality of their lives, herbs have always been a part of the story. On every continent and in every social class, people have utilized herbs to enhance their lives. Egyptian tombs, dating as far back as 2000 B.C. include evidence of anise, cumin, marjoram, and other herbs and spices. In ancient Europe, rosemary emerged as a meat preservative, while in the tropical areas of the Far East, aloe was typically used to beautify the skin. The most valued herb varieties were even used as a form of currency in some cultures.

Herbs have long been perceived as magical plants—gifts from the gods, treasure of the earth. Lucky are those who recognize their value and take advantage of all they have to offer.

The Golden Age of Herbs

In the third century B.C., the armies led by Alexander the Great brought many exotic treasures to the Greco-Roman Empire, including herbs discovered in the countries now known as Egypt, Turkey, Iraq, Iran, and Afghanistan. It took several hundred years for actual trade routes to become established, but as they did, Europeans were able to add numerous herbs, such anise, aloe, and saffron, to their collections.

In the history of herbs, big changes began to occur around A.D. 900, when East began to meet West. Around that time, a Persian doctor named Rhazes translated the works of Hippocrates, the Greek "Father of Medicine," and Galen, a Greek physician trained in Egypt. Rhazes applied what he learned in his practice in the hospitals of Baghdad, as did another gifted Persian physician named Avicenna. Medicines (which were still primarily herbal) and procedures from both cultures were gradually blended, and by the Middle Ages, a large assortment of plants had become essential medicines, as well as food flavorings and preservatives. They even had important roles in religious rituals.

When reviewing the history of herbs, it is easy to see that some people simply overestimated the power of these plants. For instance, it was believed by some that holding a sprig of bay could prevent an epileptic seizure or that a tincture made from calendula flowers could cure tuberculosis. By the time the first English-language herbals were written, people were ready to believe that herbs were cure-alls for every sickness of the body, spirit, and mind. The most popular herbal of all, *Culpeper's Complete Herbal,* published in 1651, fed this public hunger. Nicholas Culpeper's mission was to give common people the ability to see to their own health, which, in his mind, involved a combination of herbs, astrology, and faith. Most libraries still keep a copy of this phenomenal bestseller, in which herbs are prescribed for every imaginable malady and undesirable mood.

Unfortunately, Culpeper's identification of plants was often in error and

Nicholas Culpeper

A legendary figure in the field of herbal medicine, Culpeper published *The Complete Herbal* in 1651. A phenomenal bestseller, the book continues to hold a place on most library shelves today.

his cures were untested. We now know much more than Culpeper did about herbs that heal, as well as those than can cause harm. Seen as a piece of history, Culpeper's herbal makes entertaining reading. However, it may have set herbal medicine back by encouraging people to trust remedies that simply did not work and possibly made their miseries worse.

As colonists arrived in the New World, they found that Native Americans used plants both as a means of healing and as part of their religious ceremonies. Yet tribal shamans were a superstitious lot, and their art was very much a blend of effective herbal treatments and supernatural spells (see "Native American Herbs" on page 13). Due to the way herbs were mixed with magic in both European and Native American traditions, they quite logically came to be seen as less than trustworthy as the age of modern science began.

Modern Developments in Herbs

As miraculous new medicines began replacing herbs, the American way of thinking about herbs changed. Medical science was good, herbal lore was silly, and to think otherwise seemed unintelligent. A similar change occured with culinary herbs. Plenty of high-protein meat paired with potatoes became America's ideal meal, processed foods replaced those made with fresh ingredients, and using one's time to cook from scratch became an old-fashioned indulgence.

Fortunately, the unfavorable reputation that herbs developed in America did not spread to or develop independently in other parts of the world. As modern medicine came to China, it made a place for itself beside traditional herbal medicine. India, Japan, and Germany preserved herbal medicine as well. In similar fashion, chefs from Paris to Hong Kong did not abandon their ancestral roots when tempted by cake mixes and boxed macaroni and cheese.

The country's back-to-the-land movement of the 1960s led to a sudden revival of interest in all things natural, including herbs. Soon thereafter, the Internet and other advances in communication made it possible for herbal

Native American Herbs

The colonization of North America was so aggressive, bloody, and fast that pause was seldom taken to record how Native Americans used indigenous plants as medicines and foods and in their religious ceremonies. The few people who did show interest in how Native Americans used herbs met with mixed reviews. One early authority on Native American healing practices, Philadelphian Dr. Benjamin Rush, announced that the herbal knowledge of Native American healers had nothing to offer the practice of medicine. Others disagreed with this assessment, but the deep-seated belief that white men knew more than those who were native to the land won out. Desperate settlers, who often lived far from educated doctors, often did use herbs and methods shared by Native Americans. When the cures failed to work (as they often did), belief in the usefulness of "Indian medicine" weakened even further.

Although native herbs fared poorly in the field of medicine, they played an important role in North America's economic and political growth. By the late 1700s, hundreds of tons of Native American ginseng were being dug from the woods of Canada and the Appalachians to be shipped to China. Following the Boston Tea Party, colonists began drinking tea made from monad, a native plant that was cultivated by a Shaker community in New York. Many herbs, such as catnip and St. John's wort, were transported from Europe along with the colonists. They escaped gardens, and began to grow wild in the New World. In addition, the colonists discovered native species of mint, rosemary, and sage that were similar enough to the Mediterranean versions to work as substitutes in recipes for tonics, salves, and stews.

The story of Native American herbs continues. Echinacea, a Native American plant, is the most popular medicinal herb today, sold in health food stores, pharmacies, and supermarkets around the world. Goldenseal, which grows wild in shady woods, produces roots containing several compounds that work as natural antiseptics. Goldenseal's chemistry is complex and potent, so much so that its uninformed use may be dangerous. It is unfortunate that more is not known about its use in traditional Native American medicine. However, research is ongoing to evaluate goldenseal's value in the treatment of infections, hormonal imbalances, and cancer.

Clearly, North America was not left out in terms of being richly endowed with herbs of great value. Today, some of the most promising varieties being studied by scientists—for example, black cohosh—are Native American plants.

practitioners to learn how herbs are used in far-flung corners of the world with a click of a mouse. As a result, we now have unprecedented opportunities to make use of healing herbs in ways that have survived tests of time *and* scientific scrutiny, and we can follow the lead of the world's greatest chefs in using culinary herbs. Herbs also have established their value in the field of aromatherapy. Gardening has emerged as the top hobby of the early twenty-first century, so of course, growing herbs ranks high, too.

Today, we have no need to justify an interest in herbs. Indeed, knowledge of herbs has again become something that most well-informed people want and need. Herbs are back in style, but they are not just a fad. Rather, the same herbs that brought health, flavor, and pleasure to our forebears have simply made a comeback—this time with ample justification for being welcomed into our lives.

CONCLUSION

We will revisit the history of herbs as it applies to health, food, creative uses of herbs, and gardening in the next four chapters. Herbs cannot be neatly sorted into categories based on a single primary use, because many herbs are multi-purpose plants. For example, aloe, the well-known medicinal herb that magically heals minor burns, is also an easy-to-grow houseplant that removes formaldehyde from the air.

One of the lessons we learn from the history of herbs is that it is not enough to desire that these plants improve our health, flavor our foods, or make our homes more enjoyable places to live. We also need to know how to handle them, and have realistic expectations of what they can and cannot do. The next chapter takes some of the confusion out of shopping for herbal health products by giving you the information you need to be a smart consumer. Then, you'll learn how to make teas, extracts, and other herbal remedies from whole herbs that you might grow in your own backyard.

CHAPTER 2

Herbsfor Your**Health**

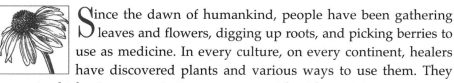 Since the dawn of humankind, people have been gathering leaves and flowers, digging up roots, and picking berries to use as medicine. In every culture, on every continent, healers have discovered plants and various ways to use them. They learned which plants cured illnesses, restored health, and, in some cases, soothed problems of the spirit. When we use medicinal herbs today, we make use of both ancient and modern knowledge of how these plants work to promote good health.

Following a quick review of the history of medicinal herbs, this chapter discusses important safety issues associated with various plants. It then explores the world of medicinal herbs as it exists today. You will learn how to choose wisely among the many available herbal products, as well as how to make your own herbal preparations for both external and internal use. Table 2.1 on page 37 will help you find the best herbal remedies for a number of common health problems.

The information in this chapter is designed to make you a smarter consumer of herbal health remedies, so that you can buy and use them with confidence.

HISTORICAL HIGHLIGHTS OF MEDICINAL HERBS

The history of medicinal herbs contains all the elements of a great story. It combines the most honored of human virtues—hope, compassion, and faith—with much less honorable ones, such as ambition and greed. Yet the story is far from simple; it is marked by huge gaps created by language barriers, religious restrictions, social conventions, and geographical distances. Still, it is only by looking at the historical evolution of medicinal herbs that we can truly appreciate the way we are able to use these plants today.

The oldest practitioners of herbal medicine were the medicine men, shamans, and village healers of prehistory. For tens of thousands of years, herbal knowledge was passed from one generation to the next, with knowledge of the most potent and dangerous of plants left in the hands of those who knew how to use them. This tradition continues in remote villages of Africa and South America, where modern ethnobotanists often brave heat, insects, parasites, and other discomforts in the ongoing search for new cures from old plants.

In terms of written history, writings made on papyrus in Egypt around 1700–1500 B.C. are among the oldest evidence of herbs being used to treat illness. In addition to herbs, ancient healing formulas included animal substances ranging from bat saliva to various parts of crocodile, as well as bits of insects and worms. It was not until the late 1800s—a time span of 3,500 years—that this ancient Egyptian lore was studied and read by Western scholars.

Ancient Egyptian writings have provided some of the oldest evidence of herb usage for treating illnesses.

The First Pharmacies

In ancient Greece, healing formulas were often based as much on hope as on results. People wanted restored health, but in an age ruled by belief in magical yet capricious gods, gullibility ran high. Legally, drug makers (known as apothecaries) had more freedom to experiment and to make promises than did physicians, who faced dire consequences, such as the loss of a hand, if they failed to bring about a cure. This separation became more defined after

Hippocrates (460–377 B.C.), the Greek "Father of Medicine," set forth the code of honor that doctors still use today.

Aristotle (384–322 B.C.) is best known as a philosopher, but he was also deeply involved in herbal medicine, and even kept an apothecary shop in Athens. He spent years helping to identify and catalog the new medicinal plants that Alexander the Great brought back from his conquests in India, Babylon, Syria, and Israel. Three centuries later, Dioscorides (A.D. 40–80), an army surgeon, added a significant chapter to medical botany by collecting more than 600 plants and evaluating them for their healing properties.

Medical quackery, by both doctors and apothecaries, was rampant in ancient Rome. Wealthy people in particular demanded exotic healing formulas, with secondary regard for whether or not they worked. But the fall of the Empire returned herbal medicine to its basics. For 500 years after Southern Europe fell to barbarian invaders, the herbal healing arts were maintained inside the walls of monasteries, which sometimes included hospital wings, medicinal gardens, and on-site apothecaries.

These were the Dark Ages, but they were not nearly so dark further East, in the area around the Persian Gulf that is now known as Iraq and Iran. The period from A.D. 850 to 1050 is often called the Golden Age of Arab medicine. Rhazes (A.D. 860–932), a Persian physician who served as the medical chief of the great hospital at Baghdad, was a great herbalist who believed that the earth contained special plants that could cure illness if only they could be found and understood. The first true pharmacies were established during Rhazes's lifetime. But again, there was a gap in time before this herbal expertise was shared with the rest of the world. Rhazes's work was not published in Latin until more than 500 years after his death, just in time for the Renaissance.

Herbal Alchemy

Europe struggled through the Middle Ages beset by terrible medical crises,

DREAM CURES
In Greece, herbs were tightly intertwined with religious healing practices based on dreams. For example, hospitalization might include going to a special temple, being thoroughly cleansed inside and out, and then fasting until dreams were received from Aesculapius, the healing god. If the patient was lucky, these dreams would reveal which healing potions were needed to bring about a cure. These potions included herbs that were brewed into teas, made into alcohol-based tinctures, or infused with oil.

EGYPTIAN PRESCRIPTIONS
The Romans so valued the new medicines discovered in Egypt that the famous Roman physician Galen (A.D. 130–200) suggested that physicians add a few Egyptian terms to a prescription to bolster the patient's confidence in the cure.

including the bubonic plague and, a few centuries later, a devastating form of syphilis that may have been brought to Italy by the sailors who had recently helped to discover the New World. Unfortunately, an herbal potion called guaiacum, made from the wood of a tropical American tree, did not cure the disease, but it became the popular cure-all miracle drug of the Renaissance anyway. The more costly and exotic a cure, the better people liked it.

Paracelsus (1491–1541) was a free thinker who vigorously criticized revered old medical practices that did not work. A deeply religious man who felt that God had equipped the world with an abundance of healing substances, Paraclesus dared to bring metals into the mix of herbal remedies. This is how tin, silver, sulfur, and other minerals entered medicine. There were many skeptics, however, who preferred to stick with plants, including many new ones that were being imported from the Americas. Tobacco, for example, was hailed as a cure for cancer, headaches, asthma, and syphilis.

Contemporary Herbal Healing

This brings us to the beginning of the age of modern science, when advances in surgery, sanitation, immunization, and bacteriology quickly left herbal medicine in the dust. By the time the twentieth century rolled around, intelligent people were expected to embrace scientifically proven solutions, which meant discarding old folk remedies that were based on herbs. In North America, this became an either/or issue. Threats from polio and other devastating diseases that suddenly became preventable thanks to modern science set up a social climate that had little respect for herbs.

However, in some parts of the world, notably China, Japan, and Germany, the use of herbs in health and healing evolved alongside mainstream medicine, much to the benefit of both. Today, health-enhancing herbs in these countries (and increasingly, in many more) retain the respect of both doctors and patients. Why? Two probable reasons. First, we have much better ways to determine if an herb is effective, and information on how herbs work is now backed up by sound research. Second, many herbal medicines are more afford-able than "space-age" drugs, and they often have far fewer side effects.

THE STORY OF AROMATHERAPY

Cave paintings in France dating back 20,000 years depict people using aro-matic plants to enhance their lives. This is what aromatherapy is all about, and aromatherapy's evolution parallels the history of medicinal herbs. The ancient Egyptians used the fragrances of herbs in religious ceremonies, and Cleopatra is reported to have had her chambers paved with fresh rose petals to help her woo Alexander. Later, in Rome, Hippocrates may have been the first physician to prescribe herbal baths and massage to help restore good health.

A flurry of research in the early 1900s brought work with plant aromas into the age of science. Inspired by the way lavender oil cured burns on his hands, the French chemist Rene-Maurice Gattefosse coined the word "aro-matherapy" as he studied the healing powers of fragrant herbs. This research was put to practical use by Dr. Jean Valnet, a French army surgeon who used herbal preparations to treat battlefield wounds and psychiatric problems.

The marriage of aromatherapy and massage is credited to Mme. Marguerite Maury, whose groundbreaking book bore the irresistible title *The Secret of Life and Youth*. Another famous pioneer in the therapeutic use of flowers, Dr. Edward Bach (1886–1936) took another approach. His work was directed toward using flower essences to improve emotional states, which he believed were where all illnesses began. Bach's "flower remedies" are taken internally—very different from mainstream aromatherapy practices, which involve working with plant aromas by smelling them or by having diluted oils rubbed into the skin.

There are many ways to interpret and apply aromatherapy, which often involves the use of essential oils—very concentrated extracts from the leaves and flowers of plants. Chapter 4 explains much more about essential oils and

FANTASTIC POTIONS
Theriac, a recipe consisting of sixty to seventy ingredients, was wildly popular from 200 B.C. until the nineteenth century. An essential drug kept in every home, theriac was believed to be able to cure everything from snake-bite to bronchitis.

Dr. Edward Bach
Recognized as the discoverer of Bach flower remedies, which are used throughout the world.

the many ways you can use them. In addition, ideas for capitalizing on the aromatic assets of herbs are included in the plant profiles in Part Two. Indulging in the pleasures of aromatherapy can be as simple as picking a leaf of mint and rolling it in your fingers. Any activity involving fragrant herbs that reduces stress or promotes happiness qualifies as aromatherapy.

HEALING WITH WHOLE HERBS

Many of the first pharmaceutical drugs were extracted from herbs, including aspirin from willow bark and digitalis (a potent heart stimulant) from foxglove. Even today, about half of all prescription drugs are based on active ingredients originally found in plants. While there is no doubt that many of these drugs are of tremendous value, we have often "thrown the baby out with the bathwater" by looking only at primary active ingredients found in plants, extracting and synthesizing them, and paying little attention to other compounds that may enhance curative powers. When you use medicines made from whole herbs, you avail yourself of the benefits of the plant as it is packaged for you by nature.

Some of the secondary compounds in herbs are called buffers, because they work like weak acids or salts that make it easier for the body to accept the primary active ingredient. Or they may be nutritional compounds, such as vitamins or minerals, that complement the health-enhancing properties of the herb. With herbs used externally (aloe, for example), natural skin conditioners are joined by enzymes that relieve inflammation. You often get more than you think with herbs, because they are equipped to help us in ways that we still may not understand.

You may be willing to accept a certain level of mystery regarding herbs, but what about your doctor? You need not turn away your doctor's expertise because you decide to use herbs to enhance your health. Instead, understand the dilemma he or she faces. Ethically, doctors must rely on hard scientific data when it comes to the medicines they prescribe, and today, much of that data is supplied by research funded by drug companies. Manufacturers of herbal health products sponsor research studies, too, but not nearly on the scale of those undertaken by major pharmaceutical companies. So, there is an information gap. Do listen to your doctor's advice, which you should definitely get if you are taking herbs in combination with prescription medications. However, once questions of drug interactions and allergic reactions have been cleared away, the safety record of herbal health products is so strong that you can make many of your own decisions about which herbs are right for you.

Practitioners of both herbal and mainstream medicine often tell their patients to change their diets, do certain exercises, or set aside time to pray or meditate as part of the healing process. Many people who use herbal health products find that the lifestyle changes they have been intending to make for a long time become easier when they adopt a more holistic view of their bodies. From making small changes, such as drinking more water, to bigger challenges, such as losing weight or stopping smoking, a whole-body approach that involves herbs, diet, and exercise is often so empowering that you can achieve lasting results that may have eluded you in the past.

PURPOSES OF MEDICINAL HERBS

So far, I've been using the terms "medicinal herbs" and "herbal health products" interchangeably, but there are differences in the purposes for which we use medicinal herbs. Generally speaking, medicinal herbs are plants that help the body do whatever needs to be done. However, we can divide them into three groups, based on their purposes: tonics, therapeutics, and adaptogens.

By definition, tonics are herbs that promote body tone, or invigorate, restore, or refresh how the body works. Often they do this nutritionally by providing vitamins, minerals, or antioxidants. Ginger is a good example of a tonic type herb, because it improves circulation and enhances the work of the immune system. Herbal teas that contain mint (which provide antioxidants)

Safety Concerns About Herbal Medicines

All of the herbal remedies described in this book are considered safe by the American Pharmacological Society, with a few caveats. First, do not exceed the recommended dosage, both in terms of how much you take each day and how long you take the herb. Second, take heed if your body sends you signals that you may be allergic or hypersensitive to the herb. Typical allergic reactions include itching, difficulty breathing, feeling hot or flushed, and nausea. I have included appropriate precautions when discussing herbs that are known to trigger allergic reactions in susceptible individuals. Also, I strongly suggest that you study the plant profiles in Part Two before you decide to use any herb as medicine. If you are taking prescription medications, get your doctor's advice before adding medicinal herbs to your plan of treatment. You certainly do not want to overload your liver, stomach, or brain with more medicines than they can put to good use.

Pregnant women and nursing mothers also need to play it safe with herbs, some of which contain plant hormones that are so similar to human hormones that they can upset the delicate balance in a body that is essentially functioning for two. Finally, if you have a history of liver problems, you should not take medicinal herbs except under your doctor's close supervision.

along with rose hips (a potent source of vitamin C) could also be considered tonic herbs.

Therapeutic herbs stimulate specific actions in the body. These are true medicinal herbs, which are used to treat distinct diseases or problems. Most healing herbs fall into this category. When you take feverfew to treat recurrent headaches or dab calendula cream on a skinned knee, you are using herbs therapeutically. Antibiotic-like herbs also fall into this category (see "Natural Antibiotics" on page 23).

The third category, "adaptogens," has been coined to accommodate herbs such as ginseng, which simply help the body *adapt* to stress. That stress might be recovering from a serious illness, driving long distances at night, or hosting a large family gathering. Some people think of chamomile as an adaptogen, too, since it has a calming effect without causing drowsiness.

CHOOSING MEDICINAL HERBAL PRODUCTS FOR INTERNAL USE

You can use the information in Table 2.1 on page 37 and the more detailed

Natural Antibiotics

Echinacea, garlic, and a few other herbs are often taken to treat infections because of their antibiotic effects. But it's important to note that these effects are quite different from those of pharmaceutical antibiotics. Pharmaceutical antibiotics work by breaking down cell walls of the invading bacteria or by interfering with the ability of the bacteria to reproduce. The leading herbal antibiotic, echinacea, works by increasing the number of white blood cells, the body's primary way of attacking bacteria. This is why it is safe to use both types of medicines together provided you take appropriate doses.

There is another difference between pharmaceutical antibiotics and herbs with antibiotic effects: We are cautioned to take antibiotics as seldom as possible to insure that we do not inadvertently turn our bodies into breeding tanks for resistant bacteria. Therefore, ethical medical practice requires that you get sick enough for your doctor to be able to make a diagnosis before antibiotics can be prescribed. With echinacea and garlic, you can begin treating yourself as soon as you notice the first symptoms—or even if you simply know that you have been exposed to an infection. Because these herbal antibiotics work by energizing the pathogen-fighting arm of your immune system, they do not stage the same setup for incubating resistant strains that can happen with pharmaceuticals. If you are taking herbs for a suspected infection, consult your doctor if the symptoms worsen or if you not see improvement within three days.

material on individual herbs in Part Two to choose healing herbs that you may want to use. But there are still questions you'll need to answer. How do you decide between tablets or capsules, liquid extracts, or teas? Should you buy medicinal herbal products, or go to the trouble of making your own preparations? Shopping for medicinal herbs can be very confusing, so the next few pages are devoted to basic consumer information.

We'll begin by surveying the choices available when buying medicinal herbs. Once you're familiar with the products you can get in stores and how much you can expect to pay for them, you will be in a better position to decide whether you want to make herbal preparations at home or simply buy them. To further help you choose between purchased and homemade remedies, information on the procedures used to extract and store herbs' active medicinal ingredients is presented later in the chapter.

Picking a Product

When you know the herb you want, perhaps you will go to a health food store or herb shop where you know there is a wide selection. There, you'll encounter shelves filled with jars and bottles. Medicinal herbs may be packaged as teas, capsules, tablets, or varying types of liquid extracts, often displayed side by side. These types are discussed below. Following this discussion, you'll learn how to assess product content.

Teas and Infusions

Tea is one of the most popular ways to enjoy the medicinal benefits of certain herbs.

Many herbal teas are available in teabags, and a few offer standardized dosing of medicinal herbs. This means you'll get a guaranteed dose of the herb's active ingredient in each cup of tea. Teas are a good choice if you intend to use the herb only occasionally—for example, when you have a cold or a scratchy throat, or if you enjoy sipping a warm cup of catnip or chamomile tea just before you go to bed. If you prefer to drink cold liquids, it's fine to allow the tea to cool completely before drinking it.

An infusion is simply a very strong tea. Historically speaking, infusions depended more on steeping time than on the temperature of the water. A tea left to brew for a long time, until the water is lukewarm, is properly called an infusion. When the plant parts used are leaves, stems, or flowers, teas or infusions will supply you with the herb's healing attributes. A concentrated tea called a decoction is made from very hard plant parts, such as dried roots. (See "What's a Decoction" below.)

Liquid Extracts, Tinctures, and Syrups

Liquid extracts are a very effective way to take highly concentrated medicinal herbs. The main advantage of extracts is that they are absorbed very quickly, beginning in the mouth rather than in the more hostile environment of the stomach. Most liquid extracts that are sold for adult consumption are what herbalists call tinctures—concentrated herbal extracts in an alcohol base. However, some liquid extracts use a vegetable-glycerin base instead. Vegetable glycerin is usually the base used for syrups, too. Most herbal extracts made for children are in this form. Almost all liquid extracts and syrups are sold in small bottles with medicine-dropper caps for easy dosing. You can take liquid

What's a Decoction?

Tough or woody plant parts that release their active ingredients slowly may be simmered into a decoction, a very concentrated tea. The ideal procedure for making a decoction is to soak the herbs (for example, dried echinacea or elecampane root) overnight and then bring the mixture almost to a boil before allowing it to cool. The strained liquid is the decoction and is taken like tea.

extracts straight, by squirting the premeasured dose into your mouth, or by mixing it with a little water, tea, or sweetened water to mask the flavor. A few herbal extracts, such as feverfew, may cause mouth irritation. If you find that you are sensitive to any extract, promptly switch to a capsule form of the herb.

Capsules and Tablets

Almost all medicinal herbs are readily available as capsules or hard-coated tablets. This is great way to take herbs that do not have a pleasant taste or when you simply want the convenience of a pill that you can wash down with a glass of water. Capsules and tablets are also an easy way to take herbs that work best when taken daily over a period of several weeks or months.

Capsules usually contain finely pulverized whole herb, which is released in the stomach within moments after you swallow it. The coating on tablets dissolves more slowly, so tablets often are preferred if you have a sensitive stomach. However, should either herb capsules or tablets make you queasy, your body may be telling you that teas or tinctures are well worth your time and trouble.

Contents of Medicinal Herbal Products

Once you've surveyed the forms represented on the herbal medicine shelf, take a deep breath and get out your reading glasses if you need them, because checking labels is a necessary part of choosing herbal health products. The following sections discuss the three main types of product contents—plain herbs, herbs in standardized dosages, and combination blends—and how they differ in potency and price.

The Plain Herb

The least expensive forms of whole herbs are capsules, extracts, and teas made from plain herbs with no added ingredients. The only quality controls used are those that the manufacturer imposes on itself, and the dosage, or amount of active ingredient present in the product, is not standardized. Rather, you are simply buying herbs by weight. Plain herb capsules are filled with dried, pulverized herb, and unstandardized extracts are made from the procedure described in "Making Liquid Extracts" on page 32. The dosage information on the package will often suggest taking several capsules or tablets at intervals during the day. This is your tip-off that the potency of plain herb products is rather low. Still, some people prefer this form because they want their herbs pure and unadulterated.

The amount of active ingredient present is usually a smaller consideration with herbal teas, which are used more casually, often on an as-needed basis. However, a few manufacturers have begun to offer medicinal teas that provide a standardized amount of an herb's active ingredient. Look for the word "standardized" on the box when choosing an herbal tea that you plan to use therapeutically.

The Herb in Standardized or Guaranteed Dosage

Although there is a movement in the industry to use the word "standardized," some companies use "guaranteed" the same way. Either word means that the actual content of the product has been carefully analyzed and adjusted if necessary to provide a standard amount of the herb, which is listed on the label along with the suggested dose. Whether in teas, tablets, capsules, or liquid extracts, these products cost more than unstandardized ones, and price varies from one brand to another. However, it is usually true that a standardized dose of a certain herb purchased as an extract costs about the same as an equivalent dose in capsule or tablet form.

Standardized products are wise buys since you know what you are getting. To save time, ask the store personnel to show you to the standardized or guaranteed products right off the bat. Many companies that sell both plain herbs and standardized products color-code the bottle caps or labels of their different product lines.

Combination Blends

If you want to take a combination of herbs for a health problem, you might consider products that contain a primary herb with other herbs added to increase its effectiveness. These products are usually labeled according to the problem they are intended to treat. For example, products based on St. John's wort, which is used to treat depression, often include the word "mood." Echinacea products, which help with colds and other infections, often say something about colds or flu. Many of these products contain standardized doses of the primary herb, along with lesser amounts of secondary herbs. This idea sounds good, but scientific studies have rarely addressed herbal combinations; therefore, you will be operating on your own herbal knowledge. Because these products have strong public appeal, they are often easy to find.

STORAGE OF HERBAL MEDICINES

There is a reason why herb capsules and tablets are not sold in clear bottles and why liquids are packaged in dark-colored glass. Light speeds up the degradation of stored herbs, so it's important to keep them in a dark place. Cool temperatures prolong the shelf life of herbs, too. You don't have to refrigerate them; just store them where the temperature seldom rises above 80°F.

HOMEMADE MEDICINAL HERBAL REMEDIES FOR INTERNAL USE

People used to make their own herbal remedies because it was the only way to get them. Now that you can buy high-quality products, the main reason to make your own herbal remedies is because you have grown the herb and have plenty of it. Of course, not every herb needs to be preserved. Some people are perfectly happy to chomp cloves of raw garlic, and fans of feverfew often fold a fresh leaf into a piece of bread and take their dose that way. But most of us would rather save our taste buds for culinary herbs and use medicinals either as herbal teas made from dried herbs or liquid extracts made from fresh ones.

Drying Medicinal Herbs for Use in Teas, Decoctions, and Infusions

When gathering and drying medicinal herbs, always work quickly and carefully to reduce the risk of losing any of the herb's active ingredients. Whether you are drying leaves, flowers, or roots, it's best to dry them in a warm oven rather than in the fresh air, which is a slower process and increases the chance of finding molds and insects in the finished product.

Begin by rinsing the herbs to clean them. Shake off the excess water and pat them dry with clean paper towels. Drying most herbs with the leaves still attached is best, and stems that are fairly equal in length tend to dry evenly. When drying flowers, snip them from the stems first. Before drying roots, scrub them well with a vegetable brush, pat dry, and then use a very sharp knife to cut them into thin slices or shreds.

Spread the prepared herbs in a single layer on a cookie sheet. Set the oven at its lowest setting, which is usually between 150°F and 200°F. Place the herbs in the oven, and then either turn off the heat or leave it on with the door slightly ajar. Ideally, you want the temperature in the oven to be about 150°F, which can be difficult to maintain. However, if you turn on the oven only once an hour for about five minutes, and use that time to turn the herbs over, most will be nicely dried in only three hours or so. Don't worry if drying seems to take longer. In the oven, it's better to dry medicinal herbs slowly rather than let the temperature get too high.

Checklist for Choosing Medicinal Herb Products

Now that you've surveyed the products available, it's time to make a final decision on which form of the herb you want to use. This decision includes several factors—convenience, effectiveness, and your personal tastes and preferences. Consider how you would answer the following six questions, and you'll be well on your way to choosing the best product for your needs.

～ Do you want fast, efficient action for an acute problem?

If your answer to this question is yes, most herbalists would suggest trying a liquid extract first. Liquid extracts are highly concentrated, so you only take a little at a time, usually only a half teaspoon. Herb extracts are not particularly tasty, so most people mix them with a little tea or sweetened water rather than taking them straight. Follow label directions for dosing, which may be measured in drops. After using a liquid extract a few times, you won't have to count drops. Instead, you can measure the right amount by using the medicine dropper, which is standard equipment in the packaging of liquid herbal extracts. Liquid extracts retain their potency for up to a year when stored in a cool, dark place.

～ Will the herb be taken several times a day or over a long period?

Feverfew, St. John's wort, and other herbs that are normally taken continuously on a long-term basis are widely available as tablets or capsules. This is good, because capsules are convenient to carry and you will need only water to take them no matter where you are. However, do not make the mistake of thinking that every herb available in this form is appropriate for long-term use. Goldenseal, for example, should not be taken for more than three days, if at all. With herbs that are taken for longer periods, such as valerian to improve sleep, remember that the higher the potency of the capsules, the fewer of them you must take. Follow label directions to make sure the dosage you take is therapeutic yet safe.

❧ How does the herb taste?

Not all teas taste good, and some extracts are hardly palatable even after they are mixed with wine (an old custom!). Capsules are the answer for unpleasant-tasting herbs, such as valerian, or those that have a very strong flavor, such as garlic.

❧ Will the herb be taken by children or elderly people?

Choose a sweetened syrup or a liquid extract in an alcohol-free base for children and older adults. There are many herbal products especially made for children, which takes the guesswork out of dosing. For elderly people, you can mix syrup or extract with almost any drink, from a liquid dietary supplement to a small glass of sherry, if appropriate.

❧ Do you enjoy drinking tea?

Tea increases your water intake, which often has therapeutic effects by itself. Many people also derive benefits from the relaxing ritual of drinking a nightcap of herbal tea or sipping a stimulating one in the morning. However, the amount of active ingredient you get in herbal tea is often modest, so tea is not the best choice if you want to take an herb to treat a persistent health problem. In addition, teas made from plant roots usually taste very earthy, which few people like. On the plus side, some good-tasting herbs, such as chamomile, fennel, and hops, which are often taken to soothe abdominal distress, usually do the best job when taken as tea.

❧ Will the steaminess of the tea be beneficial?

When your throat hurts or your nose is stuffed, drinking hot tea or sipping hot soup often makes you feel better. Hot tea also can help warm you up when you feel cold, and simply smelling hot tea may cheer you a bit as well.

Herbs are dry when most of the leaves are crisp to the touch and can be pulled from the stems with ease. Try to keep the leaves whole as you pull them from the stems, though many will crumble. Store the herbs in clean jars with tight-fitting lids. If you notice pieces that are not quite dry, return them to a warm oven before placing in the jar.

To make tea from dried herbs, place 1 teaspoon of the herb in a heatproof teapot for each cup of tea. Pour boiling water into the pot, and allow it to steep for two to three minutes. Strain into a cup, and sweeten to taste or add a squeeze of lemon juice if desired. You can make a single cup of tea by placing the dried herb in a metal tea ball, and steeping it right in the cup.

Making Liquid Extracts

Making liquid extracts takes some time, but you can expect excellent results with this time-tested method. You will have no way of knowing the potency of the extract, but most people who find themselves with a teeming bed of lemon balm, St. John's wort, or echinacea are willing to proceed on faith. When you are ready to use your homemade extract, you can always mix it with a standardized one from the store to insure its potency.

Begin by sterilizing a glass jar with a tight-fitting lid. Thoroughly wash the fresh herbs, and pat them dry to remove excess water. Chop the herbs finely with a sharp knife and place them in the jar. Pour in enough liquid (100 proof vodka or vegetable glycerin, available at health food stores) to barely cover the chopped herbs. Swish vigorously to mix, and add more liquid if needed. Screw on the lid, and place the mixture in a dark place at room temperature. Shake the jar once a day, and allow the mixture to steep for two weeks before straining it through a coffee filter into a clean glass jar. Store the extract in a cool, dark place until needed. The typical dosage for herbal extracts is a half teaspoon, taken up to three times a day, usually between meals.

MEDICINAL HERBS FOR EXTERNAL USE

Some of the most dramatically effective medicinal herbs are those that are used on the skin. For example, nobody has invented a substance that heals burns as well as the gel found in aloe leaf, and the herb arnica stands alone as a practical way to soothe overworked muscles and speed the healing of bruises. In cosmetic surgery, many patients are told to use arnica cream to make the residual bruises heal faster.

The selection of herbs for external use is quite small, just as it is among mainstream drugstore first-aid products. So shopping for these products is much simpler compared with shopping for medicinal herbs that are taken internally. As I did with herbs you might take internally, first I'll walk you through a quick survey of the products you are likely to find at a good health food store or herb shop, and offer tips for making smart choices. Later, we'll look at making the homemade versions.

Creams and Ointments

Most of the herb-based products that are used externally are sold as creams, and usually come in small tubes. Perhaps the most popular are calendula creams, which are the natural counterpart to antibiotic creams and ointments. Creams that are formulated to reduce the itch of rashes or insect bites may contain calendula, comfrey, and aloe, often with the addition of aromatic herbs, such as mint. And, if you don't keep an aloe plant handy for treating minor burns, the next best thing is to have a small tube of aloe gel, or aloe gel combined with a little lavender oil.

Your local drugstore may have little to offer to help with bruising, unless they happen to stock arnica or comfrey creams. Arnica is the real star when it comes to treating bruises and sore muscles, and many people who participate in active sports keep a tube in their gym bag. It really does work. Comfrey cream's special niche is treating minor but persistent patches of dry or irritated skin.

Virtually all drugstores sell capsaicin-based creams, which use the hot compounds in cayenne and other hot peppers to confuse pain receptors, thereby reducing pain from arthritis, rheumatism, or strained muscles.

Although highly effective, capsaicin creams must be handled with care. Wear disposable rubber gloves as you apply them, and make sure you have some milk on hand in case you find that the burning sensation is too uncomfortable. Milk is the best substance for washing off excess capsaicin. And never, ever touch your eyes, nose, or other mucous membranes when there is a chance that your hands carry even the smallest trace of capsaicin cream.

Compresses, Poultices, and Plasters

Before there were easy-to-use creams, there were three other ways that herbs were used to heal from the outside in—compresses, poultices, and plasters. These are still useful today, as evidenced by capsaicin patches that are applied to aching muscles. These patches are the latest refinement of the poultice, in which moist or chopped herbs (sometimes traditionally chewed into a wad) were placed on the sore spot and bandaged in place. If you burn your finger and place a split leaf of aloe on the burn, with a bandage to hold it in place, you have made a poultice.

Compresses combine the effects of a healing herb with hot or cold temperatures. Hot compresses (which should be merely warm, no more than 120°F) often soothe sore muscles, while cold compresses help reduce swelling. Hot compresses are sometimes combined with "warming" herbs, such as cayenne, ginger, and comfrey. Cold compresses may make use of cooling herbs, such as mint or arnica.

Plasters are similar to poultices, except the herbs used are finely ground (rather than chopped), and they may have added ingredients such as wheat flour, which adds to their cohesiveness. Before they are applied, plasters are typically placed within thin layers of material to protect the skin. They are often very strong, especially when potent herbs such as mustard and garlic are used, and can cause skin irritations. Once a standard remedy, plasters are not as popular as they once were.

The Skinny on Skin

Skin that is basically healthy and unbroken is capable of absorbing the healing properties of herbs. Topical application of certain herbal creams, ointments, and oils can be very effective in treating conditions ranging from sore muscles and joints (cayenne pepper works well) to depression and dull mental functioning (rosemary oil is recommended). Skin that is injured or broken, however, is an entirely different matter. Cuts, scrapes, rashes, and minor burns must be treated with plants such as aloe and calendula, which are natural allies of the skin's own healing capabilities. See Table 2.1 on page 37 for a listing of these and other healing herbs.

Homemade Herbal Remedies for External Use

Most commercially available topical herbal creams are very good and worth purchasing, but if you have a quantity of calendula blossoms, comfrey root, or arnica flowers at your disposal, you may want to make your own. Unfortunately, making smooth creams are difficult. It's a very messy process, and learning the proper "feel" of mixing together just the right amounts of oil and beeswax (the ingredient that is responsible for turning the oil into a cream) requires experience. Instead of making cream, consider using your herbal crop to make an infused oil. In terms of usefulness, there is no difference between these two products. And please be aware that infused oil is not the same as essential oil. An infused oil is like an herbal marinade, while essential oil comes from the plant leaves themselves. There is additional information about essential oils in Chapter 4.

To make an infused oil, begin by cleaning the herb thoroughly, which means scrubbing if you are working with comfrey roots. Coarsely chop the herb and place it in a small saucepan. Add just enough vegetable oil to cover the herbs. Turn the burner on very low heat, and warm the mixture for two hours while stirring occasionally. You can also heat the mixture in an oven set at 200°F. Watch carefully to make sure that you warm the herbs rather than cook them. Allow to cool, and transfer the mixture to a clean glass jar. Screw on the lid, and store in a cool, dark place for a week. Strain the mixture through a coffee filter into a clean glass jar, and store the infused oil in a dark place, protected from sunlight.

A warm compress is another easy-to-prepare external herbal remedy. Basically a cloth that is soaked in an herbal fluid, a compress is placed on the body and kept warm. One of the beauties of a compress is that it takes just a few minutes to prepare. First, make an infusion—a very strong tea made with an herb and allowed to steep at least fifteen minutes. Strain the mixture. Dampen a washcloth in the warm infusion, wring out the excess, then lay the cloth on the affected area. Cover the cloth with a warm dry towel. When the cloth cools, remove the compress and repeat the procedure. Continue for up to thirty minutes.

LEARNING MORE ABOUT MEDICINAL HERBS

All of the medicinal herbs that are covered in detail in Part Two are also summarized in Table 2.1 on page 37. The herbs are sorted according to their use. However, there are many more healing herbs that deserve careful consideration by anyone who wishes to use herbs medicinally, including certain tree barks, mosses, and even fruits and vegetables such as cranberry and carrot. Should your quest to use medicinal herbs take you beyond the scope of this book, always seek out the most up-to-date information you can find. Older herbals often suggest treatments that modern science has found to be dangerous, such as taking comfrey or tansy internally. And as recently as the 1970s, many books on medicinal herbs did not include plants such as echinacea and ginkgo, which we now know to be extremely valuable.

TABLE 2.I. PRACTICAL USES FOR MEDICINAL HERBS

HEALTH CONDITION	HERB	COMMON FORMS AVAILABLE
Bruises and Sore Muscles	Arnica*	Cream, ointment, liquid extract
	Cayenne*	Cream, oil, transdermal patch
	Comfrey*	Cream, bulk herb, liquid extract
Colds	Echinacea	Capsule, liquid extract (often combined with other herbs)
	Ginger	Capsule, powder, fresh root
	Horehound	Tea, syrup, capsule, liquid extract
Coughs	Anise	Seeds used to brew tea
	Elecampane	Tea, capsule, liquid extract
	Fennel	Seeds used to brew tea, capsule
	Horehound	Tea, syrup, capsule, liquid extract
Depression	St. John's wort	Capsule, tablet, tea, liquid extract
	Rosemary	Massage oil (diluted essential oil)
Headaches	Feverfew	Capsule, liquid extract, whole fresh leaves
Indigestion	Anise	Seeds used to brew tea
	Chamomile	Tea, bulk herb, capsule, liquid extract
	Fennel	Seeds used to brew tea, capsule
	Hops	Tea, bulk herb, capsule, liquid extract
Infections	Echinacea	Capsule, liquid extract (often combined with other herbs)
	Garlic	Capsule, fresh cloves
	Ginger	Capsule, powder, fresh root
	Goldenseal	Capsule, tea, liquid extract (often combined with other herbs)
Mouth Sores	Cayenne	Tea made from fresh fruit or powder, used as gargle

*For external use only.

HEALTH CONDITION	HERB	COMMON FORMS AVAILABLE
Mouth Sores (continued)	Chamomile	Tea used as gargle
	Lemon balm	Tea or infusion used as gargle, special oral cream
Painful Joints	Cayenne*	Cream, oil, transdermal patch
	Feverfew	Capsule, liquid extract, fresh leaves
	Rosemary*	Massage oil (diluted essential oil)
Poor Circulation	Garlic	Capsule, fresh cloves
	Ginger	Capsule, powder, fresh root
	Ginkgo	Capsule, tablet, liquid extract
Relaxation and Sleep	Catnip	Tea, capsule, liquid extract
	Chamomile	Tea, bulk herb, capsule, liquid extract
	Hops	Tea, bulk herb, capsule, liquid extract
	Lemon balm	Tea, liquid extract
	Valerian	Tea, capsule, liquid extract
Skin Irritations and Minor Burns	Aloe*	Fresh leaf gel, packaged gel or cream
	Calendula*	Cream, gel, infusion
	Lavender*	Oil (diluted essential oil), cream

*For external use only.

CONCLUSION

This chapter supplied you with a basic introduction to herbal medicine. Now you can begin to make use of the simplest and most effective remedies available in the herbal world. Herbs are special plants that can help keep you healthy. One way to stay well with their help is through a healthy diet. Herbs make eating well a fascinating adventure, which is the subject of the next chapter. Once you learn to use the sprightly, savory, and subtle flavors of herbs in cooking, don't be surprised if you always find yourself hungry for them.

CHAPTER 3

Herbsin theKitchen

Unlike any other human endeavor, cooking allows us to match a basic biological need—our body's requirement for food—with wonderful tastes, smells, and the soul-stirring experience of being creative. And when the intriguing flavors of herbs come into the kitchen, cooking becomes even more interesting.

This chapter is all about culinary herbs. It presents various methods for bringing out their best flavor, as well as advice on how to choose between fresh varieties and dried. For those times when you have a generous supply of herbs on hand, you'll learn how to preserve them through freezing and drying methods, and how to capture their flavors in oils, vinegars, and butters. When cooking, you'll discover which herbs combinations work well together. Rounding out this chapter are recipes for a variety of flavorful pesto sauces to toss with your favorite pasta or vegetable dishes, and a number of delicious herb-inspired dry rubs to enhance the taste of fish, meat, and poultry.

But be forewarned. Once you discover the fun of cooking with herbs, you will probably want to grow your favorites in a small herb garden or perhaps in a collection of pots assembled on your terrace or patio. Many of the most popular culinary herbs are easy to grow and require only a little space. Their preferences for soil, sun, and weather are explained in general terms in Chapter 5, and more specific growing tips are included in the plant profiles in Part Two.

CULINARY HERBS COME OF AGE

There is nothing new about cooking with herbs. In times past, herbs were mainstays in the kitchen because they easily could be grown by rich or poor, they vastly improved the flavor of wild game and earthy vegetables, and some could even preserve certain foods. Today, we use culinary herbs mostly because they taste good, but many also have tremendous nutritional value. Parsley, for example, is a powerhouse of vitamins A and C, and ginger and rosemary contain a large supply of antioxidants, which help prevent cellular damage and disease.

There is also an adventure angle to cooking with herbs. Many herbs work best when used in foods that have deep roots in far-off cultures, such as oregano in Greek or Italian food, tarragon in French dishes, or ginger in classic Asian fare. So, even if you rarely travel, you can use herbs anytime to visit distant lands. For example, I use dill to recapture recipes from my grandmother's Sweden, or team up cilantro, garlic, and cayenne for a taste of Thailand.

SMART SHOPPING FOR HERBS

Every supermarket includes a spice section that is well stocked with dried herbs. For some herbs, the dried version is just fine. Dried bay, oregano, thyme, and rosemary work almost as well as the fresh versions, and seeds that keep well for long periods, such as anise, caraway, coriander, and dill, are always dry. Dried herbs vary in how long they retain their flavor and aroma. Some last a few months, while others last for years. Because dried herbs are expensive and they don't last forever, it's wise to buy them in small containers. The best way to tell if a dried herb you have on hand is still good, open the container, give it a good sniff, and then take a taste to see if it still packs a punch.

For optimum flavor, purchase herbs that you do not use often just before you need them. And don't look for much help from manufacturers in the form of "best if used by" dates printed on the labels. Some manufacturers do put these dates on the labels (or stamp them on the bottoms of tins), but the expiration date is usually given in years rather than in months.

Many dried herbs are sold in both tins and bottles, but one type is not better than the other. It is, however, important to store herbs that are packaged in glass bottles in a dark cabinet, where they will be protected from exposure to light. Light causes the flavor compounds in herbs to break down rather rapidly. And whether you buy herbs in tins or bottles, look for whole-leaf varieties rather than those that are ground or powdered. Dried leaves or leaf flakes usually release a burst of flavor when crushed or rehydrated. With ground or powdered herbs, much of the flavor has already been released.

HERBS FOR THE WELL-EQUIPPED KITCHEN

It's always a good idea to wait until you need herbs for a recipe before buying them, but if you cook often (or plan to), there are a few herbs that deserve a permanent place in your kitchen. Among fresh herbs, some form of parsley is good to have in the refrigerator at all times. Cilantro is recommended if your menus lean toward Mexican or Asian themes. I keep fresh gingerroot in the refrigerator, too, but if I won't be using it for a while, I slice it up and store it in the freezer. And, because I'm strongly biased toward fresh garlic (as opposed to powder or salt), I keep at least one whole bulb on my countertop at all times.

A few dried herbs are so versatile that they belong in every kitchen, especially if you like to cook without a book. As soon as I run low, I restock my spice rack with the following herbs and mixtures, which I consider to be kitchen essentials because they have so many uses.

COMBINING FRESH HERBS WITH DRIED HERBS

When you are using a dried herb, such as thyme, along with a fresh one, such as parsley, place the dried herb on your cutting board and chop the fresh one with it. The flavor of the dried herb will be revived as it is chopped, and the juices from the fresh herb will help rehydrate the dried one.

- **Bay**—whole leaves are required for full, rich flavor in soups, stews, or stocks.

- **Curry**—a powdered blend of a dozen or more herbs, for rice, seafood, and potatoes.

- **Italian Seasoning**—this mixture of marjoram, thyme, rosemary, sage, oregano, and basil can be sprinkled on bread, added to butters, used in sauces or salad dressings, or tossed with hot pasta.

- **Thyme**—the go-everywhere herb, for rice, potatoes, pasta, and just about any vegetable or meat.

BUYING AND HANDLING FRESH HERBS

One of the most exciting developments in the produce sections of supermarkets is the increasing availability of fresh herbs. Fresh herbs may be sold in small bunches or enclosed in plastic bubble packs, but the packaging matters much less than the actual condition of the herbs. With "live" herbs, fresher is always better. Leaves should be well colored and free of bruises or signs of wilting. Smell the herbs if they are offered in loose bunches, and check the expiration dates on packaged varieties. Sort through the display to see if there are differences in the "best if used by" dates. Always choose the freshest package available.

As soon as you bring them home, spend a few minutes preparing fresh herbs for short-term storage. Doing so will add several days to their storage life. The following preparation method is basically the same for all fresh culinary herbs, whether you buy them in loose bunches or packaged.

First, remove the herbs from their packaging, including the rubber bands or twist ties used to secure bunches of parsley, cilantro, or mint. Quickly rinse the herbs in cool water, and discard any stems or leaves that have wilted. Shake off the water, and spread the herbs out on a clean kitchen towel. Use a second clean towel to gently dab away most of the excess water; it is not necessary to get the leaves completely dry. Check the cut ends of the stems for puckering, splitting, or discoloration. If necessary, use a sharp pair of scissors to snip off the ends until you reach fresh, unblemished stem tissue. The purpose of this step is to reopen the stem ends, giving the herbs a renewed opportunity to take up additional moisture.

Place a damp, folded paper towel in a resealable food storage bag along with the herbs. Pack them loosely, allowing a little free airspace within the bag. Then, store the herbs in the refrigerator, checking them daily and removing any stems that are wilted or dark—the first signs of deterioration. Handled this way, most fresh culinary herbs will keep nicely in the refrigerator for five to seven days—ample time to come up with plenty of great recipe ideas. The inset below provides some basic tips for harvesting the herbs in your garden.

Herbs From the Garden: Prime Picking

The best time to gather most culinary herbs from the garden is midmorning, after the dew has dried but before the hot sun causes evaporation of essential oils. When harvesting herbs for drying (or any other method of preservation), try to choose the most desirable harvest time. In terms of ideal weather, two sunny days after a deep watering or soaking rain sets the stage for leaves to be nicely plumped with both nutrients and essential oils.

For maximum fresh storage life, or to "condition" herbs before preparing them for any method of long-term storage, place the cut stems in a jar of water, and chill your freshly picked herbs in the refrigerator for an hour or two before cleaning them.

WAYS TO PRESERVE HERBS

Especially when you must buy them off-season, fresh herbs can be quite expensive. The surest way to justify their cost is to not waste a single stem or leaf that might be preserved for later use. And, if you grow your own herbs, you will certainly want to preserve your garden's herbal bounty.

Most of us think of drying as the main way that herbs are preserved, but it is only one of several methods, and drying is not appropriate for all culinary herbs. Basil and dill, for example, lose most of their flavor when dried, so freezing is a better option. When you have only a few stems of any herb, you can simply chop them into an herb-flavored butter (see page 51). The plant profiles in Part Two include the best ways to preserve individual culinary herbs, but the procedures for freezing and drying, and for using herbs to make flavored vinegars and infused oils are presented here. You can also freeze herb butters and pestos (puréed herb pastes) for up to three months, provided the proper modifications are made. These special instructions are presented in the recipes beginning on page 53.

Freezing Herbs

All of the herbs that do not dry well—and some that do—can easily be frozen for later use. Basil, dill, fennel leaves, and parsley are good candidates for freezing. I love to use frozen "chips" of gingerroot, which are easier to chop than the fresh version. Some cooks think that these and other frozen herbs will keep their flavors and colors best if you blanch them first—plunging the leafy stems into boiling water for about thirty seconds, and then into a bowl of ice water. I think this procedure does more harm than good. Instead, I suggest a much simpler method. Rinse your herbs and pat them dry, and then place them in a single layer in resealable plastic containers. If you have more herbs than will fit in a single layer, use several containers for the initial freezing, and then combine the herbs into one container after they are frozen. Another good method is to spread the clean, dry herbs on a cookie sheet, freeze them uncovered for a couple of hours, and then quickly pack them into airtight plastic freezer containers.

You can also freeze herbs by making herbed ice cubes. The herbs can be chopped or whole, and you can use juice or stock in place of water if you prefer. For example, if you want to freeze basil to use later in pasta sauces, you might chop it very coarsely, place the chopped basil in ice-cube trays, and cover it with tomato juice. Chicken stock is a good liquid to use when freezing cubes of thyme or parsley for soup. To preserve mint leaves for iced tea, it's fun to allow a single leaf for each ice cube, and cover it with a light-colored juice, such as white grape juice. Regardless of the herbs or the liquid, simply place the herbs in a clean ice-cube tray, add the liquid, and freeze overnight or until hard. Then transfer the frozen cubes to a clearly labeled freezer bag.

Drying Herbs

Most of the so-called Mediterranean herbs, including chervil, marjoram, oregano, rosemary, savory, tarragon, and thyme, are easy to dry and then store in glass jars. You also can dry mints and tea herbs, such as chamomile, as well as lavender and other herbs that are appreciated primarily for their aromas. Finally, seed-producing herbs, including anise, caraway, coriander, dill, and fennel, practically dry themselves once they reach their mature stage in the garden.

Once dried, you can store herbs in airtight containers for a year or more, either separately or in combination with other dried varieties. I have suggested several combinations in the recipes for dry rubs beginning on page 57, or you can make your own. For example, oregano, thyme, and savory make a versatile blend for Italian dishes, while a combination of dried marjoram, tarragon, and thyme provides the perfect flavor for French-inspired fare.

There are four basic methods for drying herbs: hanging, screen drying, oven drying, and drying in a microwave. I believe the two fastest methods—

oven and microwave drying—are best for culinary herbs because they are fast and exact. By using an oven, you end up with dried herbs that are never sullied by molds, mildew, or insects, which can occur with herbs that are dried by hanging or screen drying. However, if you have a large quantity of culinary herbs to dry, hanging and screen drying are worth considering. Detailed instructions for these methods are given in Chapter 4.

Oven and Microwave Drying

To dry herbs in either a conventional or microwave oven, begin by rinsing the herbs to clean them. Shake off the excess water, and then pat dry with clean paper towels. Most herbs are best dried with the leaves still attached to the stems, and they will dry more uniformly if the stems are fairly equal in length. Some cutting of stems may be needed with long-stemmed herbs such as oregano and tarragon. For example, you might cut stems into pieces 3 to 4 inches long rather than having some that are long and others that are short. As you cut the stems, also snip away any leaves that are brown, show faint webbing from spiders or other insects, or appear badly spotted by disease.

To dry herbs in a conventional oven, set the heat at its lowest setting, which is usually between 150°F and 200°F. While the oven warms, spread the groomed herbs out in a single layer on a clean cookie sheet. Place the sheet in the oven and then either turn off the heat, or leave it on with the door slightly ajar. Ideally, you want the temperature in the oven to be 140°F to 150°F, which can be difficult to maintain. However, if you turn on the oven once every hour for about five minutes, and use that time to turn the herbs, most will be nicely dried in three hours or so. It's best to dry herbs slowly rather than letting the temperature get too high. If the herbs get too hot, they will begin to cook, and you will smell their precious flavors being vaporized.

Herbs are dry when most of the leaves are crisp to the touch and can be pulled from the stems with ease. Try to keep the leaves whole as you pull them from the stems, though many will crumble. Store the dried herbs in clean jars with tight-fitting lids. If you notice pieces that are not quite dry, return them to a warm oven for a few minutes before packing in the jar.

Microwave drying is good for small batches of herbs that can be put on a plate in a single layer. This method involves barely heating the herbs, usually for only fifteen to thirty seconds (depending on your microwave oven), and then letting them cool completely before rearranging them and repeating the procedure. You will need to repeat this drying cycle several times. You may also find that the leaf tips are crisp while the stem ends need further drying. For this reason, I think it's best to switch to oven drying as the last step, so that all of the herbs dry evenly before being tucked away in jars and stored in a dark, cool place.

MAKING HERBAL VINEGARS

Matching the flavors of herbs with those of various vinegars is fun, and herbal vinegars always turn out right. There are many different types of vinegar, each

Saving Savory Seeds

Let stems of seed-bearing herbs, such as anise, fennel, and dill, ripen in the garden until the seeds begin to harden. Then cut off the seed-bearing stems and hang them upside down in a warm, airy place. To catch the seeds as they dry, place a paper bag around the seed heads and fasten it in place with a wire twist tie or string. Or you could spread newspaper under the hanging stems. After two weeks or so, the seeds should be dry, and a slight touch will cause them to fall into the paper bag or onto the newspaper. Place the seeds in a clean, dry pan, and sort through them by hand to remove any foreign material. Store them in an airtight glass jar and keep in a cool, dark place.

with differences in color and flavor. Vinegars made with savory herbs like oregano, tarragon, and garlic are often used in salad dressings. For these blends, a good wine vinegar (red or white) or a sweet, mellow-flavored white balsamic is recommended. You could also try pairing amber-colored apple cider vinegar with dark green oregano, or clear white rice vinegar with red-leafed basil. The possibilities are endless, limited only by your imagination and sense of culinary adventure.

Traditional methods for making herbal vinegar vary slightly, mostly in terms of whether the vinegar is heated before or during the marinating process. Some cooks prefer to heat the vinegar almost to the simmering point before pouring it over the herbs, while others don't heat the vinegar at all. I prefer to use warm vinegar, but the choice is yours. In order to meet with successful results, follow the simple steps described in the following basic tried-and-true method.

To make a flavored vinegar with any herb, begin with a clean glass jar and approximately two cups of fresh herbs. Rinse the herbs well, and dry them as best as you can with paper towels. If using garlic or hot peppers, which sometimes float to the top of the jar, thread them onto a toothpick. If using leafy herbs, crush them slightly in your hands before placing them in the jar. Cover with two cups of warm vinegar, and then press down the herbs with a wooden spoon to make sure they are fully submerged before screwing on the lid. Place the jar in a cool, dark cabinet for two to three weeks, shaking it every day or so to keep the herbs nicely mixed.

When the vinegar is ready, strain it through a coffee filter into pretty bottles that are sealed with corks or caps that have an inner plastic coating. Avoid aluminum-lined caps, which react adversely to vinegar. For a decorative touch, add a fresh sprig of the primary herb used for flavoring the vinegar to the bottle. Stored in a cool, dark place, the vinegar will keep for up to a year. Herbal vinegars set on sunny windowsills may look pretty, but the light will cause them to rapidly lose their flavor.

MAKING HERB-INFUSED OILS

Making infused oil is slow and messy, but if you love basil or tarragon, you will want to add this to your repertoire of preservation methods. Although you also can make infused oil with other herbs, basil and tarragon are the most popular choices.

Rinse the herbs clean, and pick enough leaves from the stems to measure between 1 and 2 cups. Place the leaves in a clean heatproof bowl and cover with boiling water. Let sit thirty seconds, and then drain. Squeeze out the excess water with your hands, and place the wilted herbs and 2 teaspoons of lemon juice in a clean glass jar. Mix well with a wooden spoon, and then add 2 cups of extra virgin olive oil. Mix again, screw on the lid, and place in the refrigerator for one week. The oil will solidify, but will melt when you place the jar in a pan of hot water. You can leave the herbs in the oil, refrigerated, for about a month. For longer storage, it's best to strain the herbs from the oil.

COOKING WITH HERBS

The flavor of herbs can be strong or delicate, and only the most robust species maintain their flavor when cooked for long periods. This is often a good thing in the case of some herbs like bay and rosemary, which are so assertive that a long simmer in a roasting pan or soup pot is necessary to make them pleasing to the palate. Then there are herbs such as oregano and thyme that impart richness and fullness of flavor when they cook down to nothing, and yet also liven up foods when used fresh. For some dishes, its fine to do both—add these herbs early in the cooking process and let their flavors mellow, and then add a light sprinkling of the fresh version to the dish just before it is served.

Several fresh herbs like basil, marjoram, dill leaves, and fennel leaves simply cook away when subjected to long cooking times. It's important to add these herbs at the last minute. As for herbs that are used as seeds, including

GARLIC OIL

If you want just a hint of garlic flavor in your salad, marinate three peeled, halved cloves of garlic in a quarter cup of olive oil for a few hours, and then pluck out and discard the garlic. Use the scented oil to make a vinaigrette or any type of dressing you prefer.

caraway, coriander, and fennel, often only a very small amount is needed. It helps to lightly toast and then coarsely crush the seeds before adding them to whatever you are cooking (see "Crush Them Kindly" below). Rather than actually infusing various dishes with their flavors, herbs used as seeds become crunchy tidbits to savor along with the vegetable, meat, or fruit that is featured in the dish.

COMBINING HERBS

Combining herbs is part of the art of cooking, and I think that it is generally a good idea to stick with only one or two strongly flavored herbs in any given dish. Of course, there are exceptions, as in two classic French combinations, *bouquet garni* and *fines herbes*. Parsley, thyme, and bay are tied together in a bunch in *bouquet garni,* which is usually used to flavor stocks, soups, and stews. *Fines herbes,* a harmonious mixture of chervil, chives, parsley, and tarragon, is often stirred into salads, sauces, and vegetables. In addition to these classic herb combinations, the pesto and dry rub recipes given later in this chapter combine a number of herbs for both their flavors and textures.

By experimenting and trusting what you learn through experience, you

Crush Them Kindly

To bring out the best in fennel, coriander, and other herbs used as seeds, toast them lightly in a dry nonstick pan over medium-low heat for about three minutes, or until you can smell their fragrant aroma. Remove the seeds from the pan before they begin to brown, and let them cool. Crush the toasted seeds with a mortar and pestle, or in a spice grinder, a small food processor, or coffee grinder. You can also simply give the seeds a vigorous chop with a heavy knife.

will quickly develop your ability to cook with herbs, and your cooking will probably be better than it has ever been. To help you along, Table 3.1 on page 52 shows what I call culinary compatibles—herbs that tend to partner well when used together. However, I don't mean that they should be used all at once. For example, when I say that dill's compatibles include chives, mint, oregano, and parsley, my intention is that you choose only one herb from this list should your dill dish need a second choice for added flavor. You can use this same trend in meal planning by featuring a certain herb in one dish and using one of its compatibles in another.

MAKING HERB BUTTERS AND SPREADS

One of the easiest and most enjoyable ways to get to know the flavors of herbs is by using them to make herb butters and cheese spreads. Some of the most popular herb choices for flavoring butter include chives, marjoram, parsley, savory, and tarragon. And you can use butter, margarine, or a half-and-half mixture of either with cream cheese. Herb butter is a tasty addition to foods like baked potatoes and steamed vegetables, as well as a flavorful spread for any type of bread. Quick and easy to make, these butters can be stored in the freezer for up to three months.

Making herb butter is easy. First, soften and mix the butter. For each half cup add 1 generous tablespoon of fresh chopped herbs and a dash of lemon juice. If you are using dry herbs or a dry herb mixture, use only $1^1/_2$ teaspoons per half cup of butter.

You can combine different herbs in butters or spreads, and even add very finely chopped garlic or onion if you like. In any case, make the butter or spread at least an hour or so before serving to allow the herbs time to develop their flavors. If you plan to freeze the herb butter, wait until just before using it to add garlic or onion. When frozen, the flavor of garlic and onion sometimes becomes overpowering or even bitter.

FAMOUS PAIRS

As you study recipes, it often becomes apparent that a single herb dominates famously delicious dishes, while a second herb provides more of a supporting role. For example, many Creole dishes rely on thyme as the dominant herb but also include cayenne pepper. In Asian dishes, ginger often gets a gentle kick from garlic.

TABLE 3.1. CULINARY COMPATIBLES

Main Flavoring Herb	Compatibles
Anise	Bay, cinnamon, and citrus flavors
Basil	Garlic, oregano, parsley, and thyme
Bay	Parsley and thyme
Borage	Dill, mint, and garlic
Caraway	Citrus flavors
Cayenne pepper	Garlic and ginger
Chervil	Chives, parsley, and tarragon
Chives	Chervil and tarragon
Cilantro (coriander)	Cayenne pepper, garlic, and mint
Dill	Chives, mint, parsley, and oregano
Fennel	Garlic, oregano, parsley, and thyme
Garlic	Basil, cilantro, ginger, marjoram, oregano, parsley, and thyme
Ginger	Cayenne pepper, chives, coriander, garlic, mint, and parsley
Marjoram	Basil, dill, parsley, and thyme
Mint	Cayenne pepper, coriander, garlic, and parsley
Monarda	Chamomile, mint, and rose hips
Oregano	Garlic, parsley, and thyme
Parsley	Cayenne pepper, dill, garlic, oregano, and thyme
Rosemary	Garlic, oregano, parsley, sage, and thyme
Saffron	Chives, coriander, mint, and parsley
Sage	Garlic, parsley, rosemary, and thyme
Savory	Garlic and parsley
Tarragon	Garlic, oregano, parsley, and thyme
Thyme	Cayenne pepper, dill, mint, oregano, parsley, and sage

To turn herb butter into a cheese spread, mix it with an equal measure of finely grated Parmesan, Asiago, or sharp cheddar cheese. Finely chopped toasted nuts or olives also make a nice addition to cheese spreads.

THE MANY MOODS OF PESTO

"Pesto" is classically defined as a sauce that is usually made with fresh basil, pine nuts, garlic, grated cheese, and olive oil. Yet innovative cooks have discovered that pesto can be made with several other herbs besides basil. You can tailor pesto ingredients to meet almost any need.

I hope you will find creative inspiration in the recipes for Classic Basil Pesto, Mint Pesto, and Oregano Pesto that follow. Then, look at "Tasty Twists with Pesto" on page 56 for more ideas on making unique and delicious pestos. Whenever you find yourself with an overabundance of any fresh green culinary herb, it's time to whip up a batch of pesto.

MINT PESTO

Try this tangy sauce with baked or poached fruits, including peaches, plums, apples, or pears. You can freeze this pesto with no modifications to the recipe.

YIELD: ABOUT ¹/₂ CUP

1 cup mint leaves, loosely packed

2 tablespoons sugar

1 tablespoon balsamic vinegar

2 tablespoons finely chopped toasted almonds

1. Place all of the ingredients in a blender or food processor.

2. Blend until nearly smooth.

3. Use immediately, or store in the refrigerator for up to three days.

OREGANO PESTO

*This is an awesome sauce to drizzle over roasted potatoes
or to toss with hot rice, pasta, or cooked vegetables
such as summer squash or tomatoes.*

YIELD: ABOUT 1 CUP

1 cup fresh oregano leaves

1 cup fresh parsley leaves

1 tablespoon lemon juice

2 tablespoons chopped almonds or walnuts

2 tablespoons freshly grated Parmesan cheese

$1/4$ teaspoon salt

2 cloves garlic, coarsely chopped

2 tablespoons virgin olive oil

1. Place all of the ingredients except the olive oil, cheese, and garlic in a food processor or blender. Pulse a few times to mix.

2. Gradually add the olive oil, blending until a thick sauce forms.

3. Stir in the cheese and garlic.* Use immediately, or store in the refrigerator for up to five days.

---

* If you are going to be storing the pesto in the refrigerator for more than five days, or if you are going to be freezing it, leave out the cheese and garlic. Add these ingredients to the pesto before using. For smaller portions, add 2 tablespoons of grated cheese and 1 clove of finely minced garlic to every 1/4 cup of sauce.

CLASSIC BASIL PESTO

This pesto is ideal for tossing with hot pasta or spreading on bread just before it's baked. You can also use it as a condiment for fresh tomatoes, soups, baked fish, or cooked potatoes.

YIELD: ABOUT 1$\frac{1}{2}$ CUPS

3 cups fresh basil leaves, loosely packed

$\frac{1}{2}$ cup fresh parsley, coarsely chopped

$\frac{1}{2}$ cup pine nuts

I teaspoon chopped oregano (or $\frac{1}{2}$ teaspoon dried)

$\frac{1}{2}$ teaspoon freshly ground black pepper

$\frac{1}{2}$ teaspoon salt (or to taste)

$\frac{1}{2}$ cup virgin olive oil

I cup freshly grated Parmesan cheese

4 cloves fresh garlic, finely minced

1. Place all of the ingredients except the olive oil, cheese, and garlic in a food processor or blender. Pulse a few times to mix.

2. Gradually add the olive oil, blending until a thick sauce forms.

3. Stir in the cheese and garlic.* Use immediately, or store in the refrigerator for up to five days.

---

* If you are going to be storing the pesto in the refrigerator for more than five days, or if you are going to be freezing it, leave out the cheese and garlic. Add these ingredients to the pesto before using. For smaller portions, add 2 tablespoons of grated cheese and 1 clove of finely minced garlic to every $\frac{1}{4}$ cup of sauce.

FREEZING PESTO

Freeze extra pesto in snack-sized resealable bags, set on a plate so they will freeze flat. Store the frozen bags inside a larger freezer bag. A flat "pancake" of pesto will thaw in about an hour at room temperature, or in thirty seconds in most microwave ovens.

Tasty Twists with Pesto

Pesto has four main components—greens, liquid, nuts, and cheese. The following information is designed to show you just how flexible and creative you can be with these ingredients.

The Greens. It's always nice to have at least a little basil in pesto, but you can use many other greens as well. Arugula, cilantro, mint, parsley, spinach, and watercress are great choices for making delicious pesto to enjoy with crusty bread, vegetables, meat, or hot pasta. When using frozen spinach, be sure to squeeze out the excess water once it's thawed.

The Liquid. If you're trying to reduce the amount of fat in your diet, you can substitute lemon juice or broth (vegetable or chicken) for some of the olive oil. If you are giving your pesto an Asian spin, reduce the salt and use a little soy sauce or tahini (sesame seed paste) in place of some of the olive oil. Walnut or almond oil can be substituted for olive oil, which is a good idea when you desire a nuttier flavor.

The Nuts. Pecans or walnuts make great substitutes for the costly pine nuts used in the traditional recipe. Almonds and hazelnuts also make interesting additions. Lightly toasting the nuts before chopping will bring out their flavor and keep them from becoming mushy. Of course, it's fine to make pesto without any nuts at all.

The Cheese. Use the cheese variable to fine-tune the spreadability of pesto. Finely grated Asiago cheese makes a smoother pesto than Parmesan, while Romano gives it a more robust bouquet. Cottage cheese, ricotta, cream cheese, or even yogurt can be added to pesto to give it a creamy texture. And, if you want a nondairy version, use either tofu or puréed cannellini beans as a substitute for the cheese.

HERB BLENDS FOR DRY RUBS

If the phrase "herb encrusted" makes your mouth water, you will love cooking with dry rubs—blends of dried herbs and spices that form a crispy crust on roasted or pan-fried meats, poultry, fish, or even blocks of tofu. These mixtures are invaluable during grilling season, and you can let them do double duty as seasonings for herb butters and cheese spreads. Use 1 teaspoon of dry-rub mixture per half cup of soft butter or butter/cream cheese mixture, and allow the spread to "marry" in the refrigerator for an hour before serving.

The blends below can be prepared in small batches and stored in a dark cabinet in airtight jars. To help them form a nice crust on juicy meats, mix 2 tablespoons of the rub with 2 tablespoons of plain flour before rubbing it on meat or fish that has been rinsed, trimmed, and patted dry. You may need more for a large roast or turkey. And you can omit the flour and simply sprinkle the mixture onto burgers or chicken just before they are pan-fried or grilled.

For a change of pace, minced garlic or freshly grated lemon peel make great last-minute additions to dry rubs. Use your imagination to create your own mixtures for original recipes.

SPICY THREE-SEED RUB

Use this rub as is, or combine it with chopped fresh herbs, like basil or garlic. Excellent with beef, pork, and most types of firm fish.

YIELD: ABOUT 1 CUP

½ cup fennel seeds

¼ cup coriander seeds

1 tablespoon coarsely ground black or white pepper

2 tablespoons salt

1. Place the fennel and coriander seeds in a dry nonstick pan over medium-low heat. Stirring constantly, cook the seeds until lightly toasted and fragrant. Remove from the pan and allow to cool completely.

2. Crush the seeds with a mortar and pestle, or in a spice grinder, coffee grinder, or small food processor. You can also chop them with a heavy knife. Stir in the salt and pepper.

3. Place the mixture in a glass jar or airtight container, and store in a cool, dry place.

HERBES DE PROVENCE

This classic mixture of dried herbs from the south of France can be used as a dry rub on meat or fish, or as a flavorful addition to bean, vegetable, or rice dishes.

YIELD: ABOUT ½ CUP

1 tablespoon marjoram

1 tablespoon chervil

2 tablespoons thyme

1 tablespoon summer savory

1 tablespoon crushed or coarsely ground rosemary

1 teaspoon tarragon

1 teaspoon mint

1 teaspoon oregano

1 coarsely ground bay leaf

1. Mix all of the ingredients together in a small bowl.

2. Place the mixture in a glass jar or airtight container, and store in a cool, dry place until needed.

COOL CARIBBEAN RUB

*The full flavors in this rub are great for anything grilled,
from chicken to veggie burgers.*

YIELD: ABOUT 3/4 CUP

1/4 cup fennel seeds

3 tablespoons thyme

2 tablespoons coarsely ground black pepper

2 tablespoons paprika

2 teaspoons oregano

2 teaspoons sugar

1 teaspoon salt

1/2 teaspoon chili powder

1. Place the fennel seeds in a dry nonstick pan over medium-low heat. Stirring constantly, cook the seeds until lightly toasted and fragrant. Remove from the pan and allow to cool completely.

2. Combine the toasted fennel with the remaining ingredients. Place the mixture in a glass jar or airtight container, and store in a cool, dry place.

FINISHING TOUCHES

When a dish features a specific herb, it's always nice to add a sprig or two as a last-minute garnish. You can also use herb blossoms to dress up any dish. The flowers of all culinary herbs are edible, although some taste better than others. Chive blossoms, for example, are justifiably famous among chefs for their beautiful blue color paired with a mild onion-like flavor. Sage also blooms blue, and many cooks tend to use the flowers of this hardy plant more often than its leaves. Basil flowers are not very colorful, but the plants produce so many blossoms in late summer, it would be a shame not to use them to accent seasonal dishes, such as pasta tossed with basil pesto, or tomatoes and mozzarella cheese marinated with basil, oil, and vinegar.

Also keep in mind that some of our favorite comfort foods, which often start out on the bland side, offer wonderful opportunities to use fresh herbs. For example, grilled-cheese sandwiches get a flavorful lift from a sprinkling of fresh dill, scrambled eggs sing in the company of chives, and marjoram mashed potatoes are simply delectable. Whether you cook only occasionally or every day, you will come to know one simple fact about cooking with herbs: It is never, ever boring.

CONCLUSION

With herbs, sometimes it's difficult to know if you are following your taste buds or your nose, because biologically speaking, these two senses are intertwined. Many culinary herbs, such as basil and rosemary, also are valued as craft herbs, which is the subject of the next chapter. If you love using herbs in your kitchen, perhaps there are places for them in other parts of your home as well, where you can appreciate them for their aromas, colors, textures, and sentimental meanings. Herbs are kitchen essentials, but there is not a room in your house that cannot benefit from the richness of herbs.

CHAPTER 4

HerbsAround the**House**

Throughout history, people have used herbs to make everyday life more fragrant, beautiful, and meaningful. In earlier times, aromatic herbs such as chamomile and mint were strewn on floors to refresh stale indoor spaces. In the humblest of homes, herbs were once used to ward off evil and bring the inhabitants good luck, while those who were more prosperous splashed themselves with herb-scented waters. When tossed into a fire, oregano and sage produce a smoldering aroma that was believed by some cultures to gain the attention of helpful forces from the spirit world.

We may live in a different world, but herbs still bring us special pleasures. Although we may not use these plants for purely practical reasons, their beauty and fragrance can certainly enhance our lives in many other ways. In this chapter, you'll learn about herbal essential oils and the various ways to use them. You'll also discover how to work with fresh aromatic herbs to create such items as ornamental wreaths, swags, and miniature flower-and-herb arrangements called tussie-mussies, which were originally used during the Middle Ages to mask unpleasant odors. Finally, you'll learn the time-tested techniques for capturing the aroma and texture of dried herbs in potpourri.

You do not need to think of yourself as a creative person to find success with the projects presented in this chapter. Something as simple as a bunch of sage stems hung from a cup hook in your kitchen will quickly convince you that herbs are ready, willing, and able to form a partnership with your creative side.

WORKING WITH AROMATIC HERBS

When an herb entices you with its fragrance, how can you preserve that pleasure so it lasts and lasts? The fragrances of most herbs wane over time, but drying them can preserve their character. And, in many crafts, the herb's aromas can be revived or reinforced by using essential oils, which are described in the next few pages.

Exactly what is an aromatic herb? Any herb that smells good! Many of the same herbs used in the kitchen or for medicinal purposes do double or triple duty as aromatic herbs. Chamomile, lemon balm, rosemary, and sage are fragrant examples. There are also herbs that are most valued for their aromatic and ornamental attributes, including artemisia, lavender, lemon verbena, and scented geraniums. Colorful blossoms from calendula, monarda, and rose are indispensable in many herb crafts, as are dried citrus peels, nut shells, and other odds and ends from the kitchen.

Most craft stores sell aromatic herbs already dried, but if you have an herb garden, you can dry your own. Using one of the methods described in this chapter, dry the herbs and then store them in plastic containers with snap-top lids. When you're ready to create something original and beautiful, your dried herbs will be ready and waiting!

USING ESSENTIAL OILS

Herbal body care, aromatherapy, and many crafts make use of essential oils, which are the actual oils present in the leaves, flowers, and sometimes roots of whole herbs. The phrase "essential oil" was first coined in the sixteenth century. What began as *quinta essentia,* or the quintessence of plants, we now call essential oils. Most health food stores and herb shops sell a large selection of essential oils, usually in small, dark-colored glass bottles. Small tester bottles are usually included in the display so you can sniff before you buy. (To discover the difference between essential oils and scented oils, see "Scented Synthetics versus True Essential Oils" on page 64.)

Unfortunately for the determined do-it-yourselfer, extracting essential oils is not a project to undertake at home. The best methods for extracting essential oils, such a steam distillation, require huge amounts of plant material and special equipment. The good news is that you can buy essential oils at health food stores or herb shops, and they will retain their aromas for many months when protected from heat and light.

Which essential oils do you need? Let your nose be your guide! I consider lavender oil a household must-have. It is the most popular herb for scenting everything from bathwater to closets. I also suggest keeping some kind of citrus essential oil on hand, such as tangerine or lemon oil, because the scent is fresh and uplifting. Rose oil is also a favorite, often used to scent floral potpourri.

Essential Oils for Massage

Essential oils are much too concentrated to rub onto your skin undiluted. If you dare to do so, a rash is a very possible consequence. Instead, dilute essential oils before using them to massage any body part in need of soothing or softening. To make massage oil, you can use either sweet almond oil (available at health food stores and gourmet shops) or unscented baby oil as the base. Add up to a half teaspoon of essential oil per half cup of base oil. By making small batches, you can change your scents often, which is part of the fun of using essential oils.

Scented Synthetics versus True Essential Oils

Many craft stores sell "scented oils," which are made from synthetic fragrances rather than whole herbs. Scented oils do, in fact, have some advantages—they are less expensive than essential oils, and many of them smell wonderful, making them popular choices for adding fragrance to potpourri and similar crafts. However, some people experience allergic reactions to the smell of scented oils, ranging from sneezing and coughing to low-grade headaches. And unlike essential oils, synthetic varieties should never be applied to the skin or added to bathwater.

Essential Oils for Bath and Shower

Adding a few drops of essential oil to warm bathwater is a quick and easy way to enjoy the fragrance of herbs in a relaxing bath. In the shower, add a few drops of essential oil to unscented liquid bath soap. Begin with only five drops or so per eight ounces of soap. If you decide you want a headier aroma, add a few more drops.

More Ways to Use Essential Oils

As you have seen, essential oils are commonly used for aromatic massage, in the bath, and to enhance the fragrance of potpourri. In addition to these popular uses, there are many other ways essential oils can add aromatic accents to your life. Try some of the following:

🌿 In your office, keep a small clay diffuser handy to hold a few drops of your favorite essential oil. Rosemary oil is believed to help stimulate thinking.

🌿 In your favorite reading space, rub a drop or two of essential oil on a low-wattage light bulb (less than 60 watts) *before* turning on the light.

The warmth of the bulb will cause the essential oil to vaporize, releasing its scent.

🐾 When hand washing delicate articles of clothing, add a couple drops of essential oil to the final rinse water. You can also place a few drops on a damp sock, and add it to your clothes dryer the same way you might use a commercial dryer sheet.

🐾 When replacing the disposable bag in your vacuum cleaner, dab a few drops of essential oil on the outside of the bag.

🐾 Keep a crumpled tissue or paper towel in the ashtray (assuming you do not use it for cigarettes) or the console compartment of your car. Every few weeks, place five to ten drops of essential oil on the tissue.

WHOLE HERBS FOR THE BATH

Whenever you take the time to soak in the tub, why not make it special? Herbs can turn an ordinary bath into an extraordinary event—one that can relax, soothe, or invigorate, depending on which herbs you use.

For a gentle steep, place a quarter cup of dried herbs or a half cup of fresh ones in a coffee filter and secure it with a rubber band. Place the packet in the bathtub while the hot water is running, and let it steep for a few minutes before you get in. Leave the packet in the tub while you bathe, and then, simply dispose of the wet packet when you are done.

You can also mix equal parts of dried or fresh herbs with oatmeal, and place the mixture on a small square of cloth such as a cotton handkerchief. If you wish, you can also add a little shaved soap to the mix. Secure the edges of the cloth tightly with a rubber band, and place it in the tub while the water is running. Then use the bag as a washcloth, rubbing it gently over your skin. The oatmeal softens and conditions the skin, while the herbs make for a rich aromatic bathing experience. When you're done, dispose of the contents of the cloth and rinse it clean.

Table 4.1 below presents a list of herbs that are popular to use in baths. Experiment with different herbs and herb combinations. You will surely discover some personal favorites.

TABLE 4.1. HERBS FOR THE BATH		
Good Herbs for a Relaxing Bath	**Good Herbs for a Stimulating Bath**	**Good Herbs for a Soothing Bath**
Chamomile	Hops	Calendula
Lavender	Lavender	Catnip
Lemon verbena	Lemon balm	Hyssop
Rose	Marjoram	Rose
Thyme	Mint	Sage
	Rosemary	Tansy
	Savory	Yarrow
	Yarrow	

CREATIVE CRAFTS WITH FRESH HERBS

While it's true that you can make lovely everlasting arrangements and wreaths using dried plant material, with herbs it's even better if you do the arranging while the herbs are fresh. Because herbs are more leaf than flower, they become quite fragile as they dry. So it's simply easier to make a wreath, bouquet, or tussie-mussie using fresh herbs, which are more flexible. The drying comes later, after the craft is assembled. If only dried herbs are available, you can use them to make potpourri or some of the other dried-herb crafts covered later in this chapter. After your masterpiece is dry, decorated, and ready to display, you can refresh its fragrance by adding a few strategically placed drops of essential oil of your choice.

Now, let's look a few specific herb crafts, beginning with tussie-mussies.

These little flower arrangements are such a fine way to introduce the symbolic meanings of herbs. How seriously you take the significance is up to you, but I think it's always fun to invite herbs into the way we communicate with ourselves and one another.

Tussie-Mussies (Nosegays)

Before the days of indoor plumbing and deodorant, the world could be a pretty malodorous place. In medieval times, herb lovers hit on the idea of making up small bouquets of fragrant herbs and flowers that could be easily carried or pinned to the wrist, and then rushed to the nose to mask unwanted odors. Over a period of several hundred years, the practice became incorporated into society, and tussie-mussies (also called nosegays) were often shared as symbols of special feelings. Rosemary for remembrance, sage for long life, and roses for love were three positive messages that might have been passed on through a tussie-mussie. Ones that were styled with tansy and pennyroyal, suggested that you wanted someone or something to go away. Some of the traditional meanings of herbs and herb flowers used in tussie-mussies are listed in "The Language of Herbs" on page 69.

The actual creation of a tussie-mussie, once considered a high feminine art, can be very simple or extremely complex. If you're a beginner, the following is a procedure that should yield good results.

Begin with a single colorful flower, such as a perfect rosebud, or a small cluster of tiny flowers, such as wild violets. Hold them together tightly, and surround them with sprigs of herbs. Then add an outer layer of a third plant with larger leaves or a slightly coarser texture than the herbs used to flank the feature flowers. Use stout thread to tie the bunch together, and then wrap floral tape over the thread. Cut a small X in the center of a paper doily (or you can use two) or a circular piece of lace, and poke the wrapped stems through. As a final touch, tie a colorful ribbon beneath the doily and let the ends dangle a bit.

SHOP THE FARMERS' MARKET

If you don't have an herb garden, visit a nearby farmers' market in search of freshly cut aromatic herbs during the summer months. Many small market growers sell their bounty this way. You can take the herbs home and use them fresh. Dry any that are left over.

If your supply of fresh herbs is limited, you can still enjoy crafting with them. Pick perfect individual leaves, and press them between the pages of a heavy book for a week or two, or until they are stiff and dry. Then arrange them in a framed collage, or use them to embellish note cards or the pages of a special scrapbook or journal.

You can make tussie-mussies using dried herbs and flowers, but fresh ones work much better. A fresh and fragrant tussie-mussie is sure to add delight to anyone's day. However, fresh flowers do wilt quickly, so you might want to leave the stems unwrapped and display these miniature flower and herb arrangements in small containers, such as old glass medicine bottles or tiny ceramic pots, for a day or two. Or go ahead and dry tussie-mussies made from fresh herbs by hanging them upside down in a warm room for one to two weeks. When making tussie-mussies that are to be dried immediately, wait until they are dry completely before adding the decorative doily and ribbon.

Herb Wreaths and Swags

Circular wreaths studded with herbs can be hung on walls, in windows, or over doors. Techniques similar to those used to make wreaths apply to creating swags—linear pieces in which herbs are entwined in braided jute or rope. Swags are commonly draped over a mantelpiece or door, or hung in a window. Both wreaths and swags showcase the textures and colors of herbs, and a gentle touch often releases a bit of fragrance. In fact, when you tire of looking at these pieces, you can crumble the herbs into a container and use them as a base for potpourri. (See "Potpourri" on page 72.)

You can make wreaths or swags with dried herbs, but fresh stems are much easier to work with since they do not break or crumble as easily. However, remember that herbs do shrink as they dry, so it's important to arrange them very densely on the form. The best procedure is to install the herbs on the form, as described below, and then let the arrangement dry for about two weeks. Once it's dry, decorate the piece with materials, such as ribbons, nuts, dried flowers, or even slices of dried fruit.

Before you get started, visit a craft store to get supplies. You will need a wreath form that is already covered with a natural material such as straw or moss, along with floral tape for binding together small bundles of herbs (usu-

The Language of Herbs

In the Victorian era, flower arrangements large and small were used to symbolize and communicate emotions and heart's desires, which often could not be spoken aloud without risk of social scandal. These notions are still of interest to us romantics, who never tire of sentimental signs.

Basil. Fidelity or love

Borage. Courage

Calendula. Peace and harmony

Chamomile. Humility, patience, or a shared wish for dreams to be fulfilled

Chives. Usefulness

Coriander. Secret value

Dill. Tranquility

Hops. Injustice

Horehound. Health

Hyssop. Sacrifice

Lavender. Distrust

Lemon balm. Sympathy

Marjoram. Happiness

Mint. Hospitality, virtue, or wisdom

Parsley. Festivity

Pennyroyal. Go away

Rose. Love

Rosemary. Remembrance

Sage. High-esteem or long life

Salad burnet. Happiness and mirth

Tansy. Hostility

Thyme. Strength and courage, or to purify or bless a place

Yarrow. Healing of the heart

ally three to five stems, depending on the nature of the plant). Also buy floral wire and pins, which you will use to attach the bundles to the form.

Where to begin? It depends on the final effect you want to achieve. If you install your herb bunches in a spiral pattern, so that the base of each bunch is covered by the tops of the next bundle, the wreath will have a strong sense of flow since all of the material is laid out in the same direction. The same applies to threading bunches of herbs onto a swag, and this is the typical way that swags are arranged.

With wreaths, you will get a very different result by layering materials—for example, by using one type of herb to dress the outside edges of your

AMAZING ARTEMISIA
Many herbs can be incorporated into wreaths or swags, including basil, bay, hyssop, oregano, rosemary, tansy, sage, and yarrow. However, for creating wreaths with a very full, lush look, herb crafters are unanimous in their high regard for various types of artemisia. Once used medicinally, these feathery plants often feature silver foliage, and some types have a fresh fragrance as well. They are by far the best herbs for beginning wreath makers to hold in their timid hands. (Artemisia is described in detail on page 113.)

wreath, a second type for the inside edges, and a third for the space in between. This circular-type pattern typically produces a very lush, robust look, giving the wreath plenty of depth and fullness.

If you're not sure, go ahead and make your herb bundles, and then lay them out in various arrangements on a table. When you find a pattern you like, transfer it to your form, and wire or pin the bundles in place.

The appearance of the wreath or swag will change as it dries, which is part of what makes this craft so much fun. Later, when it's time to decorate the piece, you may have a number of ideas. Use floral pins to install ribbons, flowers, more herbs, or dried fruits or chili peppers. With larger items such as whole bulbs of garlic or nuts, you'll need a hot glue gun to attach them to your dried wreath.

DRYING AROMATIC HERBS FOR CREATIVE CRAFTS

The end of summer means the end of crafting with fresh herbs, which is the main reason to stockpile a supply. You can arrange dried herbs in a vase or crumble them into potpourri, which can be displayed in a dish or used to fill sachets or pillows. First, let's look at some easy procedures for drying aromatic herbs. Later, I'll provide some classic potpourri recipes, as well as directions for making sachets and dream pillows—packets of herbs to slip into your pillow at night to supposedly enrich your dreams.

Drying Long-Stemmed Herbs

When gathering herbs with stems that are at least 8 inches long, the simplest way to dry them is to hang them in a dry, airy place, in bundles of three to five stems. I recommend binding the bundles together with rubber bands. The stems shrink as they dry, and the rubber bands tighten to take up the slack.

If you live in a dry climate, you may be able to hang bunches of herbs on a porch or in your garage to dry. Just be sure to choose a spot that does not get direct sun, which will cause the colors of the leaves to fade. This may also destroy the aromatic compounds in some herbs. I live in a humid climate, so I hang herbs indoors, usually on a small temporary clothesline located near an air-conditioning vent. I attach the bundles to the line with clothespins, and they are usually dry in about two weeks.

Although many people enjoy having bunches of dried herbs hanging in their houses, it's best to take them down and promptly store them in airtight containers after the drying process is complete. Otherwise, they can lose both their color and aroma. To keep things organized, use a separate container for each type of herb.

Drying Small Stems and Blossoms

A huge assortment of little herbal tidbits, from rosebuds to the flower spikes you clip from basil and mint, are easy to dry flat, by laying them out on a piece of newspaper or a drying screen. A drying screen allows the herbs to be bathed in fresh air from all sides. You can use an old window screen, or even the plastic trays with screen-like bottoms that are used to hold bedding plants. The first drying chamber I used for flat items was the dashboard of my car, which was parked in the shade. It heated up enough to promote fast drying, and kept the materials from blowing in the wind.

When drying herbs indoors on a flat surface, it's best to fluff and turn the material every day or so, to expose every part to fresh air. When the material is almost dry, transfer it to a cake pan and heat it in a warm 150°F oven for about fifteen minutes, or until the materials are very dry and nearly crisp. Then, store the dried herbs in plastic bins or glass jars until you are ready to use them.

CREATIVE CRAFTS WITH DRIED HERBS

Dried herbs that are transformed into smudge sticks, potpourri, sachets, or dream pillows make it possible to enjoy the fresh fragrances of summer all

WASH BEFORE YOU PICK

An hour or two before gathering aromatic herbs for drying, use a fine spray from your hose to wash down the plants, and then allow them to dry before picking. With herbs that are not intended for cooking, this method of cleaning is often sufficient, eliminating the need to wash the stems after they are collected.

year long. You can use dried stems, leaves, or flowers for these crafts. For added visual interest in potpourri, or for decorating wreaths or wrapped packages, don't miss the lovely textures and muted colors of the following herb flowers, which frequently are pinched off and tossed away: chives, feverfew, mint, monarda, oregano, rose, sage, tansy, and yarrow.

Herbal Smudge Sticks

The burning of sage smudge sticks—tightly bound bundles of sage—is an ancient ritual practiced by many Native American tribes. In the summer, when your sage has bloomed and is ready to be cut back, you can make your own smudge sticks to burn outdoors when spending "sacred" time on your deck or patio. Although sage is the herb of choice, many others, including lavender, rosemary, juniper, and oregano, work just as well.

To make smudge sticks, cut several pieces of newspaper into 8-inch squares. On the edge of each square, lay three or four 6-inch-long stems of sage (or another herb) together. Roll up the bunches tightly in the newspaper, like a cigar, and tie off the ends with string. Lay the sticks out to dry in a warm, dry place for two weeks. Before using, clip or untie the strings and remove the paper.

To use, light the end of a stick with a match, wait a few seconds, and then blow out the flame. Wave the stick in the air or blow on it gently to encourage it to smolder and smoke. Place the smoldering stick upright in a glass or metal container that is filled with a few inches of sand. This will hold the stick steady as it burns. You can put out partially burned sticks in a dish of dry sand.

Potpourri

The word "potpourri" usually conjures up a mental picture of dried herbs and flowers, mixed together, and displayed in a basket or bowl, but there is more to creating good potpourri than what meets the eye. It begins with a simple, three-step procedure. First, a special fixative that absorbs and retains herbal aromas is combined with essential oil and then left to infuse for a few days. When ready, the dried herbs are coated with this mixture, and then placed in an airtight container for two weeks or more. During this time, the herbs and the aromatic oil become permanently blended. After that, it's time to fine-tune the potpourri's texture, color, and scent before pronouncing it complete.

What follows is a closer look at the components of and procedure for making potpourri. Once you understand the process, there's no limit to the imaginative concoctions you can create. Sample recipes for potpourri are provided, beginning on page 75, along with some suggested ideas for using this aromatic herbal blend.

Fine Potpourri Fixatives

Craft and herb stores typically carry up to three products that are widely used as fixatives in potpourri: orrisroot, calamus root, and benzoin. The most common of these is orrisroot, which is made from a species of iris. Orris has only a slight fragrance of its own, but it magically captures and holds other fragrances. Orrisroot is sold both as a powder and in small pieces called "pearls." Although both forms are good, pearls are better. The reason? The powder leaves a faint coating on the potpourri, while the pearls appear as nondescript little nuggets.

Calamus is similar to orris, and is made from the root of a related plant called sweet flag iris. Calamus has a mild spicy scent, so it is best used in mixtures with rose or fruity fragrances.

Benzoin is the dried gum resin from a tropical spicebush that is related to witch hazel. Benzoin carries a strong balsamic scent, which is good in musky, strongly spiced mixtures, but can easily overpower delicate herbs.

To make the most of any fixative, mix a half teaspoon of essential oil with

REJUVENATING
POTPOURRI
All potpourri mixtures
lose their fragrance
after several months,
but you can refresh
them by returning the
material to a large
airtight container,
adding several drops
of essential oil, and
allowing it to mellow
for a couple of weeks.

three tablespoons of fixative in a glass jar. Screw on the lid, and allow the mixture to mingle for at least two days before adding it to your dry potpourri ingredients.

Dried Herbs for Potpourri

The most important ingredients in potpourri are the dried herbs, which are used not only for their fragrance, but for their colors and textures as well. In many ways, mixing herbs for potpourri is like cooking or painting, in that the mixture evolves as you see how different herbs look, feel, and smell when combined together. The recipes beginning on the next page are a good place to start, but choosing herbs for potpourri is definitely an area where you can let your imagination run free. If you have stored your dried herbs (in separate containers, of course), you have tremendous freedom to mix and match fragrances when you create a batch of potpourri. For added eye appeal, include other items such as tiny pinecones, decorative seed pods, cinnamon sticks, and whole spices.

Not much can go wrong when making potpourri, although it's wise to use essential oils very sparingly, otherwise they will overpower the scent of the herbs. For six to eight cups of dried mixed herbs and flowers, only a half teaspoon of essential oil (such as lavender, rose, or orange, stabilized in three tablespoons of fixative) is needed. Remember that you can't tell exactly how the mixture will turn out until it has been combined with the dried herbs and allowed to sit for two weeks. If you're not satisfied with the scent after that much time has passed, fine-tune it with more herbs or a few more drops of essential oil.

Try to keep herb leaves intact through the potpourri-making process. This makes the finished product more interesting to see and touch, and when leaves are crushed between curious fingers, additional aromas are released.

Making your own potpourri is fun and easy. The following "recipes" will help to get you started. Each blend provides a special fragrance that is sure to please.

Save Your Citrus Peels

The rinds of lemons and oranges are often packed with aromatic compounds, so they are ideal for adding to potpourri and even herbal tea. To dry citrus peel, cut it into strips about ½ inch wide, and use a sharp paring knife to shave off most of the white pith. Lay the prepared strips on paper towels in a dry place. After several days, place them in a 150°F oven for about an hour to finish drying. When completely cool, store in airtight jars. Use a blender or food processor to coarsely grind the dried peel for steeping in tea.

ROSE POTPOURRI

A perfect mixture for the bedroom.

YIELD: ABOUT 4 CUPS

3 tablespoons orrisroot, premixed with 15 drops rose oil

2 cups dried rosebuds and rose petals

1 cup dried rose-scented geranium leaves

1 cup dried lemon verbena

1. Place the orrisroot and essential oil in a small glass jar, screw on the lid, and shake well.

2. Mix together the remaining ingredients, add the infused orrisroot, and mix well. Transfer the mixture to an airtight container, and allow it to sit for two weeks.

3. Remove the amount of potpourri needed, then replace the lid to keep the remaining mixture smelling fresh and strong.

THREE-CITRUS POTPOURRI

This is a great potpourri for the kitchen.

YIELD: ABOUT 6 CUPS

3 tablespoons orrisroot, premixed
with 15 drops lemon, lime, or
tangerine essential oil

1 cup dried calendula flowers

1 cup dried lemon verbena

1 cup dried lemon balm

1 cup dried citrus-scented
geranium leaves

1 cup dried orange rind

1/2 cup dried lemon thyme

1/2 cup dried lemon rind

1/2 cup dried lime rind

1. Place the orrisroot and essential oil in a small glass jar, screw on the lid, and shake well.

2. Mix together the remaining ingredients, add the infused orrisroot, and mix well. Transfer the mixture to an airtight container, and allow it to sit for two weeks.

3. Remove the amount of potpourri needed, then replace the lid to keep the remaining mixture smelling fresh and strong.

LAVENDER POTPOURRI

*The scent of lavender is fresh and cooling—suitable
for any room in the house.*

YIELD: ABOUT 6 CUPS

3 tablespoons orrisroot, premixed with 15 drops lavender oil

4 cups dried lavender blossoms and leaves

1 cup dried peppermint leaves

1 cup dried monarda leaves and flowers

1. Place the orrisroot and essential oil in a small glass jar, screw on the lid, and shake well.

2. Mix together the remaining ingredients, add the infused orrisroot, and mix well. Transfer the mixture to an airtight container, and allow it to sit for two weeks.

3. Remove the amount of potpourri needed, then replace the lid to keep the remaining mixture smelling fresh and strong.

Sachets

If you can manage a basic stitch with a needle and thread, you can easily make your own herbal sachets to scent drawers and closets. First, cut a piece of muslin or other soft cloth into a 4-x-8-inch rectangle (or twice the size of the sachet you want to make). Fold it in half and stitch up the two sides, leaving one edge open. Turn this "pocket" inside out (so the stitching in on the inside). Make a $1/2$-inch hem on the open edge, turning it into the pocket. With a hot iron, press the hem in place, and iron out any wrinkles from the material. Fill

SACHETS
Sachets that are to be tucked into drawers are typically quite small. Those that go in closets tend to be larger and require a decorative ribbon to suspend them from hangers.

the pocket with potpourri, and sew the open edge closed. Now make a second pocket, slightly larger than the first one, using a more decorative fabric. Satin, linen, or any other material that "breathes" is fine. Don't use brocade or other thick, heavy material. Although these fabrics may look pretty, they tend to trap the fragrance of the potpourri within.

Stick very close to your personal herbal preferences when making sachets—you do not want your clothes to carry an aroma that you do not truly love. Personally, I like to make day-to-day decisions about scents, and often do not want my clothes to be scented at all. I use sachets only for clothes that are being stored for a season. The exception is my linen closet, where a lavender sachet keeps constant company with the pillowcases and sheets. And, in late summer, when I often have plenty of fresh herbs to play with, I sometimes make special sachets to carry up into the attic and hide in my empty luggage.

Dream Pillows (Sweet Pillows)

Little packets of fragrant herbs, fashioned so that they lie flat between pillow and pillowcase, have a long history of use as get-well gifts for the sick. But you need not be ill to enjoy having your nightly rest enriched by one of these dream pillows (also called sweet pillows), which releases a subtle herbal fragrance each time you move your head.

Some herbalists claim that various herbs help improve sleep or shape dreams. For example, calendula flowers supposedly promote prophetic dreams and help make dreams come true, while chamomile flowers are reputed to dispel nightmares. Mint is said to foster peaceful sleep. These are notions to prove (or disprove) through your own experience. In my trials, I have found that using dream pillows is just plain fun. They make that magic moment when my tired body settles into bed a wonderful reward after a busy day.

The suggested fabric and procedure required for making dream pillows is the same as that for making sachets (page 77). Although the herbs used to fill these pillows can be similar as well, it's important to avoid including sharp stems or anything that might go crunch in the night. And it's best to go very light on essential oils or omit them altogether. The fragrance should come from whole herbs that are crushed over and over as you sleep. One of my favorite blends includes dried rose petals, fresh or dried lavender blossoms, and dried lemon verbena. Spearmint, lemon verbena, and a little sweet marjoram also make a congenial trio for dream pillows. If deep sleep is your goal, a classic combination includes equal parts dried hops flowers, chamomile blossoms, peppermint leaves, and lavender leaves and flowers.

You do not have to actually put a dream pillow inside your pillowcase. Because I am a light sleeper, I prefer attaching it to the sheet beneath my pillow with a safety pin. I hardly notice it is there until a faint scent reminds me of my little nocturnal talisman.

CONCLUSION

From slipping a sprig of rosemary into a letter to a friend to hanging a lavender-scented sachet in your coat closet, herbs offer endless opportunities to exercise your creativity and generosity. I have barely scratched the surface of the many useful items that can be made with herbs. Crafters are always coming up with new twists. You can tap into this rich source of ideas by visiting herb fairs and specialty shops or by joining a local herb club. Many enthusiastic herb crafters share their favorite projects on the Internet. It will take only a little cyber-searching to discover many of these excellent ideas.

But be forewarned. The more you enjoy making things with herbs, the more you will want to grow your own plants in order to have plenty of raw materials. This brings us to the subject of the next chapter, gardening with herbs. For many herbal healers, cooks, and crafters, growing herbs as live plants is the first and most important step in enjoying their pleasures.

CHAPTER 5

Herbsin the**Garden**

 Many herbs are so easy to grow that even novice gardeners can expect great success with them. After all, most herbs started out as wild plants, which people gathered from meadows, woods, and riversides. Then, over hundreds (and sometimes thousands) of years, people gradually improved the vigor and productivity of herbs. Sometimes this was done intentionally, as people saved seeds from the best plants they could find and replanted them. In other situations, herbs were given a boost as they were introduced into new environments where they thrived. In North America, for example, numerous herbs that were imported from Europe during colonial times escaped from gardens and now grow wild in fields and along roadsides. Catnip, St. John's wort, and assorted mints are just a few of the herbs that made very successful transitions into the New World.

In this chapter, you will learn how to make herbs feel at home in your garden, even if space is limited to a few pots on your patio. You will get to know herbs as living objects with predictable lifecycles and easily met needs for sun, moisture, and nutrients. To add to the pleasure of growing herbs, you'll discover how to design a small herb garden that works as good as it looks. You'll also learn about the ongoing care of herbs, how to propagate your favorites, and how to bed down the most long-lived ones for winter.

Bear in mind that this is not brain surgery. Growing herbs is easy! Like all plants, herbs grow by absorbing three things—light, moisture, and nutrients. This fundamental principle of nature is very simple and should be kept in mind as you get to know herbs as living plants.

START SMALL

Growing herbs need not be a huge project, because only two or three plants of most types will provide plenty of stems, leaves, or flowers for whatever purpose you have in mind. Many herbs can be grown in containers or grouped together in a small bed. Of course, if you have plenty of sunny space and want to grow lavender for quarts of potpourri, or enough basil to last a year, you will need more plants. Still, it's always a good idea to start small by experimenting with several herbs that interest you. In all gardening, success is often a matter of discovering plants that you like and that also thrive in the site, soil, and climate that exist right outside your door. This process of discovery is most enjoyable when you concentrate on only a few new plants at a time.

THE LIFE CYCLES OF PLANTS

In the language of gardening, plants are sorted according to their life cycles. Herbs may be annuals, perennials, biennials, shrubs, or even trees. Shrubs, such as rose, and trees, such as ginkgo, don't exactly fit the general description of herbs, so I'll be sticking with the garden-sized plants.

Annuals are plants that sprout from seeds, grow to maturity, and then produce seeds before dying, all in the same growing season. Among herbs, basil, coriander, dill, and summer savory are four well-known annuals. Because annuals live such short, busy lives, they often need more water and nutrients than herbs that grow for more than one season. Moreover, they grow so quickly that many of these plants are ready to expire before the growing season has ended.

Perennials live longer than annuals, and they tend to grow slowly during their first year of life. Hardy perennials die back in winter, sometimes disappearing altogether, and then reappear the following spring. Bulb-forming herbs, such as garlic and saffron, also are perennials. Yet perennial herbs do not keep coming back forever. Many become old and woody after a few years, or they spread into clumps that may get too big for the space where they are planted. A few simple propagation techniques, which are covered later in this chapter, make it possible to keep perennial herbs such as sage and thyme happy and healthy season after season.

Some perennials, called half-hardy perennials, are grown as annuals because they cannot tolerate winter's cold. Marjoram fits into this group, as do many herbs from tropical climates, such as lemon verbena, scented geraniums, and many types of rosemary. If you can provide these herbs with just the right indoor conditions from late autumn to early spring, they can survive as perennials.

Biennials fall between annuals and perennials. Most members of the carrot family, including fennel and parsley, are biennials. These plants grow for a year, become almost dormant in winter, and then flower in their second spring. They usually die after that, although some plants may thrive for another season.

When choosing perennial herbs for your garden, it's best to select varieties according to the climate in which you live. The USDA Hardiness Zone Map on page 85 indicates the country's ten plant hardiness zones, based on each area's average winter minimum temperature and frost-free days. Most nurseries and seed and plant catalogs use these zone numbers to rate the hardiness of the plants they sell. Certain herbs may require special handling in areas with extreme climates, so it is wise to seek local expertise when making plant selections. Unusual climates affect herbs in unusual ways, even causing remarkable changes in their natural lifecycles. Do be reassured that, regardless of where you live, you will be able to find herbs that are well adapted to the conditions in which they will be grown.

ASSESSING THE SUN

Regardless of lifecycle, most herbs are sun-loving plants. Practically speaking, "full sun" is defined as at least six hours of direct sunlight each day. However, if your climate is very cloudy or just plain cold, plant the herbs in places that receive full sunlight from dawn until dusk. On the other hand, in very warm climates, full-sun herbs are usually happy with only five or six hours of sun, and they actually appreciate a little afternoon shade.

Because of the way the earth moves around the sun, sunlight is usually most abundant in sites that face south, so southern exposures are usually the best places to grow herbs. There are a few herbs, such as comfrey, ginseng, monarda, and sweet woodruff, that tolerate shade. These and other shade-tolerant herbs grow best in places that get a little morning sun, followed by shade in the afternoon. Eastern exposures are often ideal for these herbs.

If you've never thought much about the matter of exposure, spend a little time studying your yard before deciding where to do your planting. Then move on to the design ideas outlined below. If you find there is no suitable spot on the ground, look for places that offer copious sunshine where you can grow herbs in containers. I do both, growing a few herbs in a small bed, and others in pots and planters.

DESIGNING AN HERB GARDEN

Formal herb gardens often are laid out in geometric patterns, such as circles, squares, and triangles. Growing plants in a patterned design is fun, and it can be visually delightful if the garden can be seen from a high viewing point, such as a deck or second-story window.

Know Your Hardiness Zone

The U.S. Department of Agriculture has divided North America into ten plant hardiness zones, which are based on the average winter minimum temperature and the number of frost-free days. The map below shows these zones and lists the average minimum temperature for each. Find your zone on the map before choosing perennial herbs for your garden. Most seed and plant catalogs use these same zone numbers in rating the cold hardiness of the plants they sell.

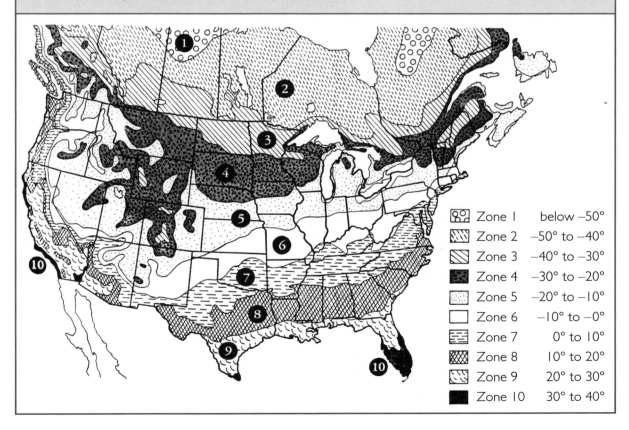

	Zone	Temperature
	Zone 1	below −50°
	Zone 2	−50° to −40°
	Zone 3	−40° to −30°
	Zone 4	−30° to −20°
	Zone 5	−20° to −10°
	Zone 6	−10° to −0°
	Zone 7	0° to 10°
	Zone 8	10° to 20°
	Zone 9	20° to 30°
	Zone 10	30° to 40°

Most herb lovers begin with more modest aspirations, such as growing a few select herbs in an informal bed or collection of containers. (See "Growing Herbs in Containers" on page 90.) If your herb collection will be viewed from one side, place the tallest plants in the rear so that each plant can easily be seen and touched. This guideline applies to both beds and containers, and benefits plants by ensuring that each one gets a full quota of light.

Beyond this practical consideration, you can be endlessly creative in how you arrange your herb garden. The following design tips can make your garden more attractive and easier to maintain.

- **Maximize contrast.** Placing plants that have very different colors and textures side by side creates a riveting visual effect. For example, purple basil and the soft gray leaves of sage make a great combination. Curly parsley planted at the feet of broad-leafed borage is another stunning partnership.

- **Group like plants together.** Growing plants in clumps or drifts makes them easier to care for, and often looks natural, as if the herbs planted themselves.

- **Plan ahead for easy access.** Don't let anything stand between you and your herbs! Include pathways or steppingstones so that you can reach every plant at any time, even in muddy weather. If you will be mowing around your herb garden, plan pathways that match the cutting width of your mower.

- **Soften the edges.** Use low-growing plants or those that spread to dress the edges of beds and containers. Intermittent clumps of dwarf curly parsley or cascades of lemon thyme are great for this purpose.

- **Include a focal point.** If possible, plant your garden around an interesting focal point, such as a birdbath, sundial, or gazing ball. Although the best focal points add vertical interest, a small concrete statue tucked among the growing herbs can also offer charm in small spaces.

MAKING A NEW HERB GARDEN

Herbs absorb moisture and nutrients through their roots, which function best in soil that has a light, fluffy texture. Clay soil is very heavy and compact by nature, while sandy soil is extremely light and porous. The difference is in the size of the soil particles. Clay particles are tiny, while sand particles are very large. Between these two types is what is called "good garden loam"—soil that contains soil particles (either clay or sand), organic matter, and a good amount of air.

To transform any soil into good garden loam, you will need to add organic matter and air. Organic matter, also called humus, is any plant material that has decomposed, such as rotted leaves, compost, or composted manure. Garden centers and home-supply stores sell bags of ready-to-use organic matter, which may be labeled as compost, organic matter, soil conditioner, or humus. These products are very inexpensive, and they are the easiest way to improve the texture of soil.

How much do you need? If you are starting a new herb garden in soil that has never been cultivated, measure the space you plan to use, then measure the length and width of the bags. Buy enough so that when you lay the bags over the space, they almost cover it. Then do exactly that. Lay the bags on the ground and use a sharp spade to cut a large X in the center of each one. Flip the bags over, dump out the organic matter, and spread it with a rake. This layer of organic matter should be at least two inches deep. Now you are ready to dig.

Use a spade or a tool called a digging fork to dig the soil at least twelve inches deep, turning, pulverizing, and mixing in the organic matter as you also pluck out weeds and roots. As you work, you will constantly be adding air to the soil. Digging when the soil is reasonably dry is also important, because wet soil squeezes together rather than crumble into pieces. You will probably need to turn the soil about three times to thoroughly mix in the organic matter and break up clods.

FRONT-ROW SEATS
Place herbs you plan to pick often in the front rows of the garden, so they are easy to reach. Also, reserve special places for very touchable fragrant plants. For instance, if you grow your herbs in containers, placing the more fragrant ones on a raised platform will bring them closer to your hands (and nose).

By the time you are finished, the bed will be slightly raised, both from the addition of the organic matter and the incorporation of air. If you like, this is the time to install a frame to create a permanently raised bed. Brick, stone, or concrete blocks make a nice frame, as does wood. I think the best choice is "plastic" lumber, which is made from recycled plastic and sawdust, and most often used to build decks. This plastic lumber doesn't rot like wood, yet it can be cut to length, just like wood. Do not use treated wood to frame an herb bed. The chemicals leach out over time, and you don't want to eat basil that has been sipping up chemicals intended to kill termites.

Checking the Soil's pH

After you have dug your herb garden and amended the soil with organic matter, check the soil's pH level, which you can do in a few minutes using an inexpensive test kit from a garden center. The pH is the relative acidity or alkalinity of the soil, which influences a plant's ability to take up soil-borne nutrients. The actual pH scale is numerical, with acidic soil reading low (usually 4.0 to 6.0) and alkaline soil reading high (above 7.5). Between these readings is the slightly acidic or near neutral range (6.0 to 7.0)—the range most herbs prefer. You can raise the pH of acidic soil by mixing in lime, which is sold as powder or pellets. Small amounts of soil sulfur, sold as a powder, will lower the pH of alkaline soil. If your herbs seem unhappy, recheck the soil's pH after a month, and make further adjustments if needed. You do not need to worry about adjusting the pH of bagged potting soils, because this has already been done for you at the factory.

NUTRITION FOR HERBS

Soil that has a light, fluffy texture and a near neutral pH gives herb roots the environment they need to absorb water and nutrients, but it may not contain

What Does "Well-Drained Soil" Mean?

Whenever you read about growing herbs, the phrase "well-drained soil" turns up again and again. This means that water moves through the soil easily rather than pooling up around the roots of the plants. Low places and compacted spots that stay muddy for a long time after it rains are not well drained. However, beds that have been deeply cultivated and enriched with organic matter usually provide very good drainage. If you think an herb needs even more help in the drainage department, mixing a few handfuls of sand into the root zone will usually do the trick.

enough nutrients to meet their needs. This is the job of fertilizers and plant foods, which are one and the same. Fertilizers come in various forms, including granular types, pellets, and those that are mixed with water and fed to plants in liquid form. You can also choose between fertilizers that are synthetic or organic. I prefer organic fertilizers, which are made from natural ingredients, but in all honesty, I don't think that my herbs can tell the difference. If they are hungry, they are just as happy with a nice slurp of blue tea, made from one of the leading mix-with-water fertilizers, as they are with the brown tea I make with its organic counterpart, fortified fish emulsion.

Most herbs do not have big appetites, so their fertilizer needs are modest. Because products vary so widely in their potency, always follow the application rates given on the label, or use slightly less than the recommended amount. Granular and pelleted fertilizers should be thoroughly mixed into the soil prior to planting. Liquid plant foods can be poured on later or used on an as-needed basis. Plants that have green leaves and show steady new growth are usually amply supplied with nutrients. Those that grow very slowly or have yellowish leaves may be underfed.

GROWING HERBS IN CONTAINERS

Herbs grown in containers need excellent soil, because their roots do not have the option of wandering about in search of moisture and nutrients. Always use the best potting soil you can find, and experiment with different brands. With potting soil, you usually get what you pay for.

There is a growing trend in the potting soil industry to include fertilizer in the blend. When using one of these products, you will not need to feed your plants for about a month after they are planted in pots. However, each time you water your plants (which may be every day in hot weather), some of the fertilizer in the soil will dissolve and run out of the bottom of the container. The more you water, and the larger plants grow (an indication that they are making use of nutrients), the more you should supplement them with additional fertilizer. Most people use liquids or water-soluble powders to feed container-grown herbs because they are easy, convenient, and make it possible to respond quickly when plants show slow growth or yellowing leaves, the two most common signs that they need to be fed.

Choosing Containers

Any container used to grow herbs must have drainage holes in the bottom, but the containers themselves may be made of clay, plastic, or a number of other materials. The most time-consuming aspect of growing herbs in containers is keeping them well supplied with water, so it's wise to choose containers with watering in mind. Large containers retain more water than small ones, and plastic holds water much better than clay. So, from a practical point of view, large plastic containers are a good choice for growing herbs. Color counts, too, in that dark-colored containers absorb more solar warmth than light ones. So, cool-climate gardeners may opt for black or dark-green containers, while warm-climate gardeners are better off with lighter colors.

The shape of the container doesn't matter, although those that are narrow at the bottom and broad at the top are prone to topple over when the plants growing in them become large. This is one reason to put a few small but heavy rocks in the bottom of containers. They add weight where it counts and help improve drainage a little, as well.

Container Combinations

It's easy to grow several herbs together in sizeable containers, such as large pots or even half barrels. One good design strategy is to use at least three plants—a tall one as the central element, a mound-forming plant to grow at its feet (usually off to one side), and a low trailing plant near the edge for visual balance. The planting will look fuller and more lush if the plants are close together, but remember that crowded plants need extra water and fertilizer.

Begin by planting the largest plant in the center or slightly to the rear of the container if it is to be viewed primarily from one side. Then, work your way outward toward the edge. In the suggested groupings below, plants are listed in proper planting order, from upright, to mounding, to trailing.

- Sage, curly parsley, lemon thyme
- Purple basil, chives, mint
- Rosemary, chervil, dill, catnip
- Lemon verbena, lemon balm, lemon mint, lemon thyme
- Basil, parsley, marjoram, thyme
- Basil, dill, summer savory

WORKING WITH SEEDS AND PLANTS

Growing herbs from purchased plants is easy and convenient, and there are several practical reasons to buy perennial herbs this way. The seeds of most

CONTAINER COMMUNITIES

Group containers close together to make them easier to water. When pots are placed shoulder to shoulder, they also shade each other slightly, so they do not dry out as quickly on hot days.

BUYING LOCAL HERBS

Does your town have a local herb society? If so, you can probably locate a contact person through your Cooperative Extension Service (look in the phone book under county services). Ask about any local greenhouse growers who specialize in herbs—the best place to do hands-on shopping for plants. There are also many excellent mail-order sources for seeds and plants. (See the Resources section, beginning on page 229.)

perennial herbs are very tiny, so growing seedlings to planting size is a slow, tedious process. Bedsides, perennial herbs grown from stem cuttings often are better plants. This is because the selected parent plants are superior in some way—for example, they may be hardier, better tasting, or more vigorous than the same species grown from seed. In addition, well-rooted perennial herb plants are ready to grow the instant you plant them.

There are also good reasons to start some herbs from seed, especially annuals. By the time annual herbs grow large enough to look good in a pot, they are often on the verge of flowering—despite the fact that they may be growing in cramped quarters with restricted roots. If you grow your own seedlings of dill, basil, coriander, or most other annual herbs, you can set them out at a very young age, or perhaps sow the seeds directly in your garden. Annual herbs that get an early start in the garden always grow better than seedlings that have waited for many weeks on garden-center shelves.

In the individual plant profiles in Part Two, you'll learn whether it is best to start each herb from seed or from purchased plants. Handling purchased plants is a simple matter of watering them well, slipping them out of their pots, and popping them into their prepared site. But as you will see, there is more involved when you're working with seeds, which can be a very rewarding way to wait for the coming of spring.

Starting Seeds Indoors

To get a jump on spring, you can start some seeds indoors in late winter—the best approach with slow-growing perennial herbs and annuals that prefer cool weather.

When starting seeds indoors, use small containers such as peat pots or paper or Styrofoam cups. Use a pencil to punch drainage holes in the bottoms of the containers, fill them with seed starting mix (see margin note on page 93), and dampen well. Wait at least an hour for the mix to become thoroughly moist.

Then, plant the seeds by barely covering them with the moistened medium. To retain moisture, enclose the containers in a loose plastic bag. As soon as the seeds sprout, which usually takes about five days or so, remove the bag and move the seedlings to a place where they will get very bright light. For steady growth, a fluorescent light fixture installed a few inches above the seedlings is ideal.

If too many seeds germinate (more than three in a two-inch-wide container), use tweezers to pull out the extras and throw them away (they are too fragile to transplant at this time). When the seedlings have three or four leaves, begin feeding them with a liquid fertilizer, mixed at half the rate recommended on the package. You can move most seedlings outdoors when they are about eight weeks old. Avoid transplanting delicate seedlings on bright sunny days. Cool days that are overcast, or early evenings are less shocking to the plants, which must adjust to their new environment. To further help them make this transition, cover the seedlings with a cloche—a glass or plastic dome that serves as a miniature greenhouse. Cloches are designed to protect seedlings from the cold, wind, and heavy rain, especially during the first two weeks after transplantation. Although you can purchase cloches at most garden centers, you can just as easily make your own from clean plastic milk cartons—simply cut off the bottoms and cover the seedling with the tops.

Sowing Seeds in the Garden

As the last frost passes in the spring, you can sow the seeds of perennials and annuals directly in your garden. There is one major drawback to simply sowing seeds where you want the plants to grow—weeds! By the time the soil is warm enough to promote good germination of herb seeds, weed seeds are also sprouting everywhere. Until the seedlings are big enough to compete with weeds, you have no choice but to help them out by pulling every little weed that crowds their space. This can be very difficult if you don't know how to tell an herb seedling from a weed seedling.

SEED STARTING MIX
Newly sprouted seeds and stem cuttings are susceptible to fungal infections, which cause them to rot. You can reduce this risk (and improve germination and rooting) by using a special medium called "seed starting mix." The leading national brand, Jiffy Mix, is a blend of finely ground peat moss and vermiculite. Look for this or similar products near the seed rack at garden centers, and use it like potting soil for starting seeds or rooting stem cuttings.

To simplify this task, you can scoop out little pits of garden soil, fill them with potting soil, and sow the seeds in these special places. Or, you can plant your seeds in a pattern, such as an S curve or a zigzag line. Hopefully, most of the seeds you plant will sprout, and you'll be able to tell from your planting pattern that they are indeed coriander, dill, or parsley. You can further confirm their identity when you thin the plants, which is almost always necessary when you grow herbs from direct-sown seeds. Thinning seedlings, by pulling out plants that are simply too close together, is often a frightening task, especially after you've waited anxiously for those seedlings to appear. But thin you must, so that each plant has at least eight inches of space between its crown and that of its closest neighbor. Some herbs need even more room than this, particularly those with large, broad leaves such as borage. As you pull out the extra seedlings, you can stop to taste and smell them. This is how you will know, definitively, that they are herbs rather than weeds.

WATER AND MULCH

During the first few weeks after planting, while herbs are beginning to grow a strong network of roots, they benefit from soil that stays evenly moist, but not extremely wet. In fact, it's usually best to slightly underwater herbs rather than give them too much water. Too much moisture in the soil, accompanied by wet leaves and humid air, can lead to problems with disease. Watering early in the morning is ideal since the water has time to soak into the soil before the day heats up, and leaves dry faster than they would if watered in the evening. However, during very hot weather, evening watering has the advantage of giving plants a long time to take up moisture before they must face another scorching day. The only time not to water herbs is in the middle of a hot, sunny day. Water droplets that heat up in the sun can actually cause burn spots on leaves.

You will not have to water as often if your herbs are mulched. A one-inch-deep layer of any mulch material, including straw, hay, grass clippings, pine needles, wood chips, sand, or pebbles, forms a buffer zone between an herb's shallow roots and the drying effects of the sun. Mulch also discourages weeds from growing.

Just be careful not to overmulch herbs. Although you may use a two-inch-thick mulch beneath the shrubs in your yard, herbs grow best when tucked in with only half that amount. The exception to this guideline comes in winter, when you may need to pile extra mulch over dormant perennial herbs to protect them from the cold. Wait until the plants have died back and the weather has turned cold to mulch over dormant herbs. Remove the winter mulch first thing in spring.

PROPAGATING PERENNIAL HERBS

There are three basic ways to propagate perennial herbs: digging and dividing, rooting stem cuttings, and layering. The method of choice depends on the natural growth habit of the plants. The most common propagation methods used for individual herbs are presented in Part Two. Here, I will explain how to perform each technique.

Digging and Dividing

Herbs that grow into clumps that become a little larger each year, such as artemisia, lemon balm, monarda, and all members of the mint family, are prime candidates for digging and dividing. How often you need to dig and divide clump-forming herbs varies with climate, but every three years is a good rule of thumb. The best time to dig and divide herbs is early spring, as soon as the plants begin to emerge from winter dormancy.

Before you dig up established herbs or remove them from their pots, have a place prepared where you can replant them right away. You can replant herbs in the same place they grew before, but if you do, refresh the soil with a two-inch-deep layer of compost while the herbs are out of the ground. If it's not practical to replant the dug herbs right away, you can plant them in pots and move them to their new home a few weeks later.

Begin digging from outside the clump by prying up the soil beneath the plant. Go all the way around the clump with a spade or digging fork. Then, lift out as much of the clump as you can, and drop it into a wheelbarrow or onto a tarp. Use pruning shears to cut away old, woody parts or spots that appear to have rotted. Replant healthy pieces of root with buds of new growth that are poised to emerge. You should see vigorous new growth within two weeks after the herbs are replanted.

Rooting Stem Cuttings

Rooting stem cuttings is an operation you can do again and again if you want to keep a perennial herb, such as lavender, sage, rosemary, or thyme, for many years. You also can root stem cuttings from mints, scented geraniums, or even roses. This technique can be a lot of fun, although you should realize from the outset that only about half the cuttings you "stick" will "take." The others will rot. So, if you want to have two plants, take four cuttings. If they all work, you will have extras to give away.

Select a healthy-looking stem tip that is not extremely woody, and cut it just below a node (the place where leaves are attached). With some herbs, such as lavender, the most rootable cuttings include a "heel"—the juncture where the stem is attached to a larger one. Instead of using scissors to gather heeled cuttings, tear them from the plants by pulling downward. Whether you take a normal stem cutting by simply clipping off a stem tip (from a mint, sage, or scented geranium) or a heeled cutting (from lavender or rosemary), a four-inch-long piece is the perfect size.

The next step is to pinch off all of the leaves except a small tuft at the tip end. Unless the herb has very small narrow leaves, such as lavender, limit the number of leaves left intact to about five. After the cuttings are groomed, stick them into a well-dampened rooting medium, such as Jiffy Mix seed starter, pure vermiculite, or a half-and-half mixture of clean sand and pulverized peat moss. Be sure the medium is nicely damp before adding the cuttings. I usually place three cuttings in a four-inch-wide pot.

Move the container to a warm spot, but out of direct sunlight. Setting it atop an appliance that warms up frequently—a hot water heater, clothes dryer, or even a television set—is recommended. To maintain a humid environment, enclose the container in a large clear or opaque plastic bag. Because you don't want the bag to touch the cuttings, placing a chopstick or skewer upright in the container will hold up the bag to form a "tent." After the first week or so, remove the bag and continue to water as needed to keep the soil moist at all times.

Allow at least three weeks for the rooting process to begin. Some plants take a little longer. Very slight new growth is the first sign that roots are beginning to form. When you see this, move the cuttings to better light and begin feeding them with an all-purpose plant food, mixed at half the rate recommended on the package. Dispose of cuttings that appear dead, and prepare places in pots or beds for your new plants. Most plants are ready to be transplanted six to eight weeks after the cuttings were set to root.

Layering

Layering is a propagation method that enables roots to develop on a stem that is still attached to the "mother" plant. It's the safest way to grow rooted pieces of herbs that become woody over time, such as lavender, English thyme, winter savory, and tarragon. However, this operation must be carried on in summer, while the plants are green and growing.

Carefully bend one of the plant's long, healthy, flexible lower branches downward until a small section of the branch (about three inches from the tip) reaches the ground. This section will be buried in the soil and left to root. Remove the leaves from this section, and bury it in a small, inch-deep hole in the ground, carefully bending the tip end of the branch upward so that it protrudes above the ground. (See the figure below.) Secure the prepared stem into the hole with a small stone or a U-shaped wire (a bent paper clip is fine), and then cover it with soil. (Scratching a small slit on the underside of this section before burying it will help promote rooting.) Cover the area with mulch to keep it moist.

Wait a month or so before gently lifting the stem to see if it has begun to develop roots. When the roots are at least two inches long, it's time to sever the stem from the mother plant and transplant it.

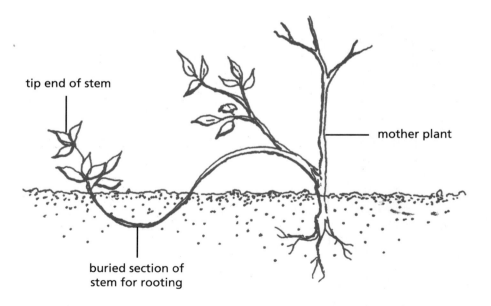

tip end of stem

mother plant

buried section of
stem for rooting

Layering Technique

PESTS AND OTHER PROBLEMS

Healthy herbs usually prosper with few problems, but sometimes there is trouble even in paradise. Problems usually are due either to insect pests, which are easily seen, or to more mysterious diseases, which can affect leaves, stems, or roots. In both cases, it's important to realize that all pests are plant-specific. Insects can digest only tissues or sap from certain plants, and diseases that infect one species of plant are very seldom able to spread to plants of a different species. So, the colorful caterpillars you find munching on your parsley (actually the larvae of swallowtail butterflies) could not devour your basil even if they were starving. Similarly, the patches of powdery mildew you see on the leaves of your monarda will never appear on leaves of dill. This is because the enzymes used by the monarda powdery mildew fungus to weaken cell walls is useless on nearly every plant except monarda.

Insect Interventions

Most herb gardeners prefer to grow plants that are free of pesticide residues, particularly herbs that are to be eaten. Large insects, such as leaf-eating caterpillars, can be hand-picked and dropped in a jar of soapy water where they will quickly drown. With smaller insects such as aphids (little wedge-shaped insects that congregate on stems and leaves) or whiteflies (tiny white gnats), insecticidal soap is usually very effective. Available at all garden centers, insecticidal soap kills insects by coating them with fatty acids without leaving behind toxic residue. In a pinch, you can spray bug-ridden plants with a mixture of one teaspoon of dishwashing liquid and a quart of water.

Dealing with Spots and Rots

When a plant begins to shrivel up and die for no apparent reason, it has probably been infected with a disease that has caused its roots to rot. Many fungi live in healthy soil, and if conditions are just right, a few soil-borne varieties are capable of colonizing on plant roots. There is no cure other than to start over with a new plant in a new place. You can grow plants in soil in which an herb died of a root rot disease as long as the new herb is not related to the one that that died. For example, if basil dies from root rot (which it occasionally does), it's okay to plant parsley in its place.

Other fungi cause diseases on plant leaves, such as powdery mildew (which looks like white, dusty patches) and a number of diseases that cause darker-colored patches or spots. Plants that are old and weak are much more susceptible to these and other diseases than young, healthy ones. The first thing to do when you see what looks like disease on plant leaves is to prune off the affected stems and dispose of them. To further protect the plant, spray it with a product that contains neem, a natural substance derived from the neem tree. Check the product label for this ingredient. Also make sure the label says the product is safe for use on vegetables. Fungicides and other pest-control products that are approved for use on vegetables also can be used on herbs.

KEEPING HERBS THROUGH WINTER

The first hard freeze of winter, in which temperatures drop into the low twenties for more than a few hours, usually causes the stems and leaves of herbs to wither and die. But only an inch or two below the ground, the roots of hardy perennial herbs remain alive although they are now in a resting state, called dormancy. If dormant herbs are covered with an insulating blanket of snow, or a thick pile of mulch, they will rest comfortably through winter and emerge anew in spring. There is nothing you must do beyond trimming off dead stems and marking the plants' locations so that you do not accidentally dig them up. Where winters are mild, for example, those in Zones 7 and 8 (see "Know Your Hardiness Zone" on page 85), many hardy perennial herbs remain green through the winter, although they show little new growth.

Perennial herbs grown in containers become dormant, too, but they are at increased risk of cold injury because their root zones are not insulated by surrounding soil. Left out in the open, repeated cycles of freezing and thawing can damage them badly or kill them altogether. For this reason, even if the herbs you are growing in containers are rated as being hardy in your area, it is wise to move them to an unheated garage, against the wall of your house, or to another cold yet protected place.

Keeping Herbs as Winter Houseplants

What about perennial herbs that cannot tolerate hard freezes, such as marjoram, scented geraniums, and lemon verbena? If you plan ahead and root stem cuttings taken in early summer, you will have small plants to keep indoors in containers. They can then be transplanted to the garden in spring. But if mature plants are all you have, dig them up, plant them in pots, and prune them to about half their size. Then try to keep them alive indoors (a cool basement is a good place) by giving them a little water from time to time. In late winter, move the plants to a warmer spot with good light, and begin giving them a little plant food. With luck, a few new stems will pop out along the base of the old ones. These can be cut and rooted as new plants, or you can move the old plant back to the garden for another season of growing.

If herbs are expected to actually grow indoors in the winter, they will either need a very sunny window (meaning one that faces south or west), or supplemental light. Most people who keep serious herb collections indoors in winter place them on a shelf under a fluorescent light fixture. If you buy an inexpensive fixture, make sure to get a size that matches the dimensions of full-spectrum "grow-light" replacement tubes, which are widely available at home-supply stores.

The culinary herbs that cooks most want, basil and parsley, can be grown indoors under lights. But even under ideal conditions, they often deteriorate

GROWING CHIVES
To have fresh chives in January, grow a nice clump in a pot, and leave it outdoors through early winter, so that the tops die back and the plants become dormant. Bring the container indoors in January and place it in good light. Fresh green growth should appear within a few weeks. Pop off individual leaves as you need them in the kitchen.

after a few months. For best results, begin with young, vigorous plants, such as seedlings started in August. But don't expect to find them at garden centers at that time of year. You will need to grow them yourself. Small perennials such as thyme and rosemary are easy to grow indoors in winter provided they receive plenty of strong light.

CONCLUSION

Growing herbs does involve an investment of energy, but this effort is paid back with huge dividends. As part of the patient process of growing herbs, you are constantly reminded of other virtues that can be learned from plants, such as adaptability, endurance, and service. And, because herbs are such forgiving plants, with the strong constitutions of the wild things that they are, you need not worry that failure will take the fun out of your first herb-growing projects. When you feel the urge to grow an herb, do it. Buy a small plant at a garden center, bring it home, and pop it into a pot or bed. There it will be for weeks to come, ready to delight you with its colors, fragrance, and perhaps flavor. And even if you've been growing herbs for years, trying one or two new ones each season will add to your enjoyment.

If you read books the way I do, you've already been flipping to the next section, studying herbs that you might want to in your garden. Perhaps you've already seen that more gardening tips await, including ideas for pairing particularly comely herbs with colorful flowers. You will also find honest information on herbs that are very difficult to grow unless they are in just the right climate. Still, expect to find dozens of tempting candidates that will enrich your garden for many seasons to come.

Essential**Herbs** from**A**to**Z**

Introduction

Herbs are unique plants with diverse talents. In Part Two, you will meet fifty-five herbs, which have been selected based upon their popularity, usefulness, and, in some cases, the need for accurate information on how they can be best used. This collection spans the entire spectrum of herbs—from those used to heal bruises, such as arnica, to herbs that do double duty as edible ornamentals, like chives and thyme. Many have been part of humankind's treasure chest of plants for thousands of years. In each entry, meaningful historical lore and knowledge gained from modern science are interwoven to give you information that is inspiring, thorough, and safe.

Arranged alphabetically by common name, these profiles summarize the main uses for the herbs, which may be medicinal, culinary, aromatic, or ornamental. Many herbs fill more than one need, which is part of what makes working with them so fascinating. Calendula, for example, is a beautiful garden flower that also has skin-healing properties, and its bright yellow-orange petals can be used in foods as an inexpensive alternative to saffron.

Most of these herbs can be grown in a garden, but several important medicinal herbs, notably ginkgo, ginger, and ginseng, are best purchased at an herb shop or health food store. For those herbs that are as pretty as they are useful, suggestions for partnering them with other plants in the garden or for growing them in containers is included under the "Ornamental Uses" heading. The "Family Relations" information which is included in many of the herb profiles, will help you get to know tasty or beautiful cousins of some of the best-known herbs. For example, you will find Japanese horseradish, or wasabi, described as part of the horseradish family, and Hamburg parsley, which produces a thick edible root, listed along with the better-known forms of this everyday herb.

The Name Game

The botanical names of plants are Latin, and they are usually composed of two words. The first word, which is always capitalized, is the name of the plant's genus. Plants in the same genus are genetically and structurally similar. The second word, which usually begins with a lower-case letter, is the species. Plants of the same species may differ in color and appearance, but genetically, they are very similar, rather like brothers and sisters.

In the world of herbs, two species names often appear: *officinalis* and *vulgare*. Herbs that bear the species name *officinalis* or *officinale* are the strain believed to be best for traditional medicinal uses. *Vulgaris* or *vulgare* means the "common" form of the plant, as opposed to other forms that are less well known.

Beyond genus and species, some herbs are available as named varieties, for example 'Munstead' lavender or 'Moss Curled' parsley. Varieties are special strains that have been selected or developed in order to feature certain characteristics, such as color, flavor, cold hardiness, or tolerance to disease. A good analogy can be borrowed from apples. There are big differences in color, texture, and flavor between 'Golden Delicious' and 'Rome' apples, but they are still very much apples. In basil, the leaves of 'Purple Delight' are dark purple, and 'Genovese' leaves are bright green, but they are still the same species, *Ocimum basilicum*.

Herbs can be used to enhance your health, flavor your food, beautify your garden, or captivate you with their wonderful aromas. Experiment with different herbs as well as their uses, and don't be afraid to include kitchen herbs in your potpourri. Part Two includes hundreds of tried-and-true ways to use herbs, although you are likely to come up with your own ideas. From slipping a snip of blue borage flowers into a glass of lemonade to sticking a stem of fresh rosemary behind your ear to help you think, the list of neat things you can do with herbs is truly endless. I hope you will use the information in this section of the book to jump-start your own imagination. After all, just because people have been eating chives for 5,000 years does not mean that every idea for using them has already been explored. With herbs, new creative opportunities are always close at hand.

ALOE

USES: medicinal

BOTANICAL NAME: *Aloe barbadensis, Aloe vera*

OTHER COMMON NAMES: burn plant

AREA OF ORIGIN: Africa

The use of aloe to nourish the skin goes back to Mesopotamia (an ancient region of southwest Asia), and it's said that one of the reasons why Alexander the Great invaded the Socotra Islands (south of Yemen) was to provide Cleopatra with aloe. The leaf juices have important medicinal uses that are more fact than folklore, making aloe one of the most respected medicinal plants in Nature's pharmacy. Although aloe looks like a cactus, it is actually a member of the lily family. A tender tropical, aloe is easily grown as a houseplant. Scientists have found that potted aloe plants also have the unique ability to remove formaldehyde from tainted indoor air.

Medicinal Uses

Aloe's talent for healing minor burns is so well known that wise cooks keep a plant within easy reach. As soon as you suffer a burn, break or cut off an outer leaf, split it open with your fingernails, and press or squeeze the leaf gel onto the burn. Repeat the application as often as needed for soothing relief. In addition to relieving pain, aloe gel reduces inflammation, works as a topical antibiotic to prevent infection, and increases blood flow to the affected area to promote fast healing. With very minor burns and sunburn, prompt treatment with aloe often leads to complete healing within one day.

You also can use aloe to treat rashes and other minor wounds, including acne and oral canker sores. Always use a fresh leaf, because the active ingredients lose potency within six hours after the leaf is plucked from the plant. Some people also take aloe internally to enhance intestinal health, usually by drinking commercially prepared aloe juice bought at a health food store. Taken in moderation, according to label directions, aloe may help heal weak spots on intestinal walls. But if aloe is consumed in excess, or if you ingest any plant part other than the clear inner leaf gel, it can cause cramping and diarrhea.

Growing Your Own Aloe

Aloe is one of the easiest houseplants to grow. The plants prefer rather dry conditions, so clay pots filled with a gritty potting soil are ideal. Aloe makes most of its new growth from spring through autumn, and many people place their plants outdoors during summer months, in a place that receives a half day of sun. In summer, water aloe plants regularly, but allow the soil to dry out almost completely between waterings. From spring through autumn, feed plants every two weeks with a mix-with-water all-purpose plant food. In winter, aloe plants kept indoors near a sunny window do not need to be fed and require only occasional water. Plants are often semi-dormant in winter, showing little, if any, new growth. They should not be exposed to temperatures below 40°F.

In summer, healthy aloe plants often develop small offshoots called pups, which pop up just outside the base of the mother plants. These can easily be cut away with a sharp knife and promptly planted into small pots. Mature aloe plants rarely bloom, but when they do, the solitary spikes feature spectacular tubular flowers in yellow and orange.

ANISE

USES: medicinal, culinary, aromatic, ornamental

BOTANICAL NAME: *Pimpinella anisum*

OTHER COMMON NAMES: aniseed

AREA OF ORIGIN: Egypt

An ancient herb cultivated in the Middle East for thousands of years, anise has a nutty licorice-like flavor. Both the leaves and seeds are edible, although it is the seeds that are generally thought of as anise. Early Romans used anise medicinally for everything from bad breath to epilepsy. They also used the seeds in sweet cakes and other treats. A strangely diverse herb, anise also finds favor among dogs for its scent.

Medicinal Uses

A tea made from steeping 1 teaspoon of anise seeds in a cup of boiling water for ten minutes can be used for two medicinal purposes—to settle the stomach and prevent gas after a large meal, and to soothe a persistent cough. To mellow the licorice-like flavor of the tea, sweeten it with honey and sip it slowly. In India, sugar-coated anise seeds are often chewed after a meal, both to aid digestion and to sweeten the breath. Because anise seeds contain anethole, a plant hormone similar to human estrogen, women who are pregnant or nursing should avoid them.

Culinary Uses

Anise leaves can be chopped into salads, or try adding young chopped leaves to creamy cucumber salad dressings. Breadsticks rolled in crushed anise seeds just prior to baking are delicious, as are crunchy cookies seasoned with anise seeds. Anise is often paired with carrots or other root vegetables. However, the most famous culinary use of anise is as a flavoring for sweet liqueurs such as French *pastis* and Greek *ouzo.*

Aromatic Uses

Many dogs like anise the same way that cats like catnip, although their response is less spectacular. But dogs often do seem to be pleased in a comforting way by the scent of anise. Tuck a small packet of anise seeds under your dog's blanket to make it a more attractive place to curl up and sleep. Folklore suggests that a small dish of anise seeds, placed on a bedside table, also encourages sweet dreams in humans.

Ornamental Uses

This dainty member of the *Umbelliferae,* or carrot, family bears clusters of tiny white flowers that seem to attract small beneficial insects to the garden while repelling houseflies. The plant's airy, fernlike blossom clusters make good filler material in cut arrangements. Try growing small groups of three or more anise plants near colorful calendulas, or use them as a backdrop for a planting of parsley or marjoram.

Growing Your Own Anise

A thrifty, slow-growing annual, anise has a delicate taproot, which makes it difficult to transplant. Sow seeds in late spring in a sunny, well-drained spot, where you can provide water during dry weather. Add lime to acid soil, because anise likes a neutral to slightly alkaline pH. (See "Checking the Soil's pH" on page 86.) Young leaves resemble flat-leafed parsley, but the leaves become much thinner and feathery as the plants grow to their mature size of 18 to 24 inches. In late summer, after the flowers fade and stems begin to turn yellow, cut the seed heads and hang them in small bunches to dry. Enclosing the bunches in paper bags, or drying them over newspapers, makes the seeds easy to gather. One well-grown plant will produce about 2 tablespoons of dried seeds. To kill any insects lurking in the harvested seeds, freeze them for a few days before storing them in airtight glass jars.

TASTY TAXES
In ancient Rome, citizens could pay their taxes in anise seed, which the government used as an international currency.

ARNICA

USES: medicinal

BOTANICAL NAME: *Arnica montana, A. chamissonis*

OTHER COMMON NAMES: leopard's bane, mountain tobacco

AREAS OF ORIGIN: Swiss Alps, Siberia, Western mountains of North America

Arnica is not well known in gardens, but this alpine herb has a long history of use in the folk medicine of Russia and the Swiss Alps, which are home to the best-known species, *Arnica montana.* Its North American counterpart, *Arnica chamissonis,* shares similar chemical properties, including the rare ability to reduce bruising and ease the pain of overworked muscles. Today, many plastic surgeons recommend that their patients use arnica creams to reduce post-surgical bruising, and athletes often carry a tube in their gym bags to soothe sore muscles.

Medicinal Uses

Most health food stores and herb shops sell arnica creams, gels, and ointments, which are made from bright yellow arnica flowers. You can also buy the dried flowers and use them to make a strong tea, or infusion, to use as a compress on bruises or injured muscles. The fresh or dried flowers also can be used to make an infused oil, which is then rubbed on to bruises. (See "Homemade Herbal Remedies for External Use" beginning on page 35.)

For best results, begin treatment with an arnica preparation soon after an injury occurs. With bruises, arnica is thought to absorb hemosiderin, a blood component that makes bruises look black and blue. Used according to label directions, which is typically twice daily, arnica cream, ointment, compress, or oil can help bruises heal in half the time it normally would take. Some people do have allergic reactions to topically applied arnica. Stop using an arnica preparation if a rash develops, and never apply it to broken skin.

Because this herb can be very dangerous when swallowed, the internal use of arnica is controversial. It is a very strong diuretic, and contains the compound helenalin, which can cause heart palpitations, coma, and even death. However, the safety record of externally applied arnica is extremely strong.

Growing Your Own Arnica

Hardy to Zone 3 (see "Know Your Hardiness Zone" on page 85), both of arnica's medicinally useful species are best adapted to cool climates or high elevations. European arnica (*A. montana*) needs acidic soil that retains moisture well. American arnica (*A. chamissonis*) grows well in alkaline soil. Both species benefit from abundant sunshine, yet they often struggle to grow in warm, humid climates.

You can start with either seeds or plants. Plants will give you a full season's head start. Mature plants form a low rosette of green foliage, from which

1- to 2-foot-tall stems emerge in midsummer, topped with yellow daisylike flowers. For medicinal purposes, collect flowers on a dry day as soon as they open, and dry them on screens or sheets of paper. Once established, arnica plants usually prosper for several years.

ARTEMISIA

USES: aromatic, ornamental

BOTANICAL NAME: *Artemisia annua, A. ludoviciana*

OTHER COMMON NAMES: ghost plant, sweet Annie, white sagebrush, wormwood

AREA OF ORIGIN: Europe

ARTEMISIA'S FAMILY RELATIONS

The genus *Artemisia* includes French tarragon, a delicious culinary herb. Many semi-wild strains of artemisia find their way into herb gardens, where they often become too invasive. Mugwort (*A. vulgaris*) is one such aggressive strain.

Named after Artemis, the Greek goddess of hunting who loved all wild things, artemisias are members of a very large plant genus that includes many highly refined garden plants with soft gray foliage, as well as a few weeds. Two species deserve a place in gardens tended by people who love making herbal crafts—the hardy *Artemisia ludoviciana*, silvery of leaf with a fine, feathery texture, and the less cold-hardy but much more fragrant *Artemisia annua*, which is often called sweet Annie and usually grown as an annual. Either species makes a fine addition to potpourri, and both are considered indispensable in making herbal wreaths.

Aromatic Uses

The most fragrant artemisia, annual sweet Annie, lives up to its name with its fresh, sweetly scented foliage. The leaves and stems are green during most of the season, and gradually turn yellowish and finally a rich red-brown in autumn. Gathered in summer, you can use the fresh leaves to make wreaths, or dry them for use in potpourri or sweet pillows. Dried stems are excellent for use in everlasting arrangements.

Ornamental Uses

Robust and persistent, named varieties of *A. ludoviciana* such as 'Silver King' are the favorite plant of herbal wreath makers. The leaves are not aromatic, but they always keep their fresh good looks when dried. Use freshly cut stems to make wreaths and swags, and then allow your creation to dry before adding more decorative touches. This plant's gray foliage is always welcome in the garden, where it helps offset potential color clashes between vivid orange or magenta flowers.

Growing Your Own Artemisia

Both types of artemisia thrive in rich, moist soil in full sun. The annual form grows quite tall, to 6 feet when planted in early spring, so it is best situated behind smaller plants. New plants must be started from seed each spring, but if you allow mature plants to shed seeds in late summer, you may discover plenty of volunteer seedlings the following spring. With 'Silver King,' begin with a purchased plant, set out in early spring, or ask a friend for a rooted piece dug up from the base of an established clump. After a year or two in the garden, 'Silver King' will grow into a robust mound 2 to 3 feet tall and equally wide. Hardy to Zones 4 to 8 (see "Know Your Hardiness Zone" on page 85), plants often grow so well that they spread into adjoining areas. Should this happen in your garden, dig up the unwanted plants in spring, pot them, and share them with friends.

SUPER SILVER FOR POTS

For herb gardens that are limited to containers, 'Silver Mound' artemisia (*A. schmidtiana*), with its feathery gray-green leaves and compact stems is a good choice.

BASIL

USES: culinary, aromatic, ornamental
BOTANICAL NAME: *Ocimum basilicum*
OTHER COMMON NAMES: sweet basil
AREAS OF ORIGIN: Africa, Asia, India

The signature herb of summer, basil is perhaps the only culinary herb that smells as good as it tastes. Basil has stirred people's passions for many millennia. It has been associated with emotions ranging from love to hate, and has been used ceremonially "to pave the way to both heaven and hell." Not surprisingly, admiration for this delicious and aromatic herb eventually won out over ancient fears of its mystical powers. Fresh basil has a seductive allure that is really quite special (no preservation method comes close to adequately capturing its flavor). Basil lovers can't seem to get enough of it.

Culinary Uses

Fresh basil is closely associated with Italian food, including pasta and tomato sauce, although it also has deep roots in Thai and Indian cuisine. Contemporary basil-crazy cooks find places for it everywhere, and there is no argument that basil's unique flavor pairs well with most hot or cold pasta dishes, cooked or fresh tomatoes, and many vegetables, including eggplant, peppers, asparagus, beans, and most varieties of squash. One of basil's quirky characteristics is that it quickly loses its flavorful taste and bouquet when cooked. For this reason, it should be added to a dish or sauce at the end of cooking time, or even used raw. Pesto—a thick puréed sauce made of fresh basil leaves, olive oil, garlic, and nuts—is one widely accepted way of making good use of copious supplies of this herb. Many gardeners freeze small containers of pesto in summer,

BASIL SEEDLINGS
When buying basil seedlings, you can sample a leaf before deciding to choose a certain variety for your garden. You can also grow a small collection of different basil types.

BASIL'S FAMILY
RELATIONS
Of the dozens of basil
species, a few carry
scents of cinnamon,
lemon, anise, and
camphor. All are fun
to grow, but the best
culinary types are
the sweet basils
(*O. basilicum*). When
growing basil from
seeds, be aware that
different species
cross easily and seed
mislabeling sometimes
occurs.

when the plant is most abundant. Another great way to capture basil's magic is by freezing basil cream sauce—a basic "white" or béchamel sauce that is seasoned with chopped fresh basil. Thawed and reheated, basil cream sauce is great with pasta, potatoes, poultry, and just about any vegetable you can name. Using the fresh leaves to make basil-flavored vinegars and infused oils is another way to sustain this herb's flavor during the off-season. You can also preserve individual leaves by freezing them. Place the clean, dry leaves in a single layer on a cookie sheet and place in the freezer. Once the leaves are frozen, quickly transfer them to a plastic airtight container, and store in the freezer. Although the flavor of frozen basil doesn't compare to fresh, popping a frozen leaf or two into a simmering sauce or adding them to cooked vegetables is still worthwhile. Dried basil, on the other hand, is weak-flavored and a very poor substitute for fresh.

Fortunately, you can usually buy fresh basil year-round at large supermarkets. Store extra stems in roomy plastic bags in the refrigerator. Basil blackens when frozen, bruised, or cut, so handle it carefully at all times. Frozen basil looks quite dark when it thaws, but it's still fine to use in cooking.

Aromatic Uses

The rich aroma of basil often envelops the garden on a warm summer day. In India and Africa, people sometimes rub handfuls of basil on their skin to repel insects. The flower spikes, which appear at the stem tops, must be pinched off often to encourage new growth. When dried, these spikes can be added to potpourri. If dried on screens and handled gently, they will maintain their green color.

Ornamental Uses

Basil comes in dozens of forms, all of which are attractive to the eye. Yet three forms are especially valuable in painterly gardens—small-leafed "globe" or "ball" basils, which are suitable for edging beds; dark-leafed "red" or "opal" basils, which have dark maroon leaves; and "ruffled" basils, with large serrated leaves that are almost lettucelike in texture. All of these are edible, although serious basil lovers often name small sweet-leafed types as having the best flavor. By growing several basil varieties, you can enjoy the beauty of this herb, while exploring its subtle flavor differences.

Growing Your Own Basil

A warm-weather annual, basil can be grown only in the summer garden. You can start seeds indoors a few weeks before the last frost, or simply buy seedlings when you are ready to plant in late spring. Whether in beds or containers, basil requires warm, well-drained soil. In cool climates, the plants must have full sun, although partial afternoon shade is welcome in areas where summers are long and hot. Small globe basils usually grow less than 12 inches tall, while larger varieties may reach 3 feet in height when in full flower.

To support basil's fast growth, beginning in early summer, fertilize your plants every two weeks with a mix-with-water all-purpose plant food. It is also crucial to pinch plants back regularly once they grow 6 to 8 inches tall. This will help induce branching—a joyous job since each time you pinch, you get more basil to bring into the kitchen. As summer wears on, continue pinching stem tips often to delay the onset of flowering. If your plants get away from you and cover themselves with flower spikes, cut off all the spikes and fertilize the plants. Within a week or two, you should see a fresh crop of new stem tips emerging.

Basil dies at the first hint of frost, but the plants may remain fragrant for several weeks afterward, reminding you of the pleasures of summer when the world is aglow with autumn.

MYSTERY WILT
When healthy basil plants suddenly wilt, the problem may be a soil-borne fungus called *Fusarium*, which injures the roots and main stem. There is no cure, but 'Nufar,' a hybrid basil, has shown resistance to this disease.

BAY

USES:	medicinal, culinary, aromatic
BOTANICAL NAME:	*Laurus nobilis*
OTHER COMMON NAMES:	bay laurel, Grecian bay
AREAS OF ORIGIN:	Southern Europe, Western Asia

In the Greek myth of Apollo and Daphne, Daphne was transformed into a fragrant and beautiful bay tree as a way of escaping from love-struck Apollo. This was bay's beginning as a symbol of greatness and nobility, and why garlands of this herb have been worn as a sign of honor by kings, poets, and athletes ever since. Actually a shrubby tree, bay is most often grown as a houseplant. A reliable evergreen, bay is always willing to give up a few spicy leaves for savory soups, stews, and sauces.

Medicinal Uses

Although bay is most often used in cooking, historical lore suggests that its oil can soothe aching joints as well as an upset stomach. However, its potency for these applications has never been formally evaluated, and the essential oil of bay can cause a rash when applied to the skin of certain individuals. Because bay contains antibacterial compounds, it is sometimes found among the ingredients in natural toothpastes.

Culinary Uses

Bay has a sharp, strong flavor, which is why only one or two leaves are needed to impart a savory richness to stocks, soups, stews, tomato aspic, and various sauces. Bay is ideal for dishes that simmer for a long time, and its subtle flavor combines easily with those of other herbs. When using fresh leaves, include only half as many as are called for in a recipe, particularly in late summer, when bay leaves taste especially strong. Always remove bay leaves before the dish is served to keep unsuspecting diners from accidentally choking on one that is sipped up with their soup.

To dry your own bay leaves, place them between the pages of a heavy book, and leave them for two to three weeks. Then store them in airtight glass jars.

Aromatic Uses

Bay plants are often pruned into symmetrical shapes. Trimming yields short stems studded with fragrant leaves that can be used fresh, perhaps in combination with seasonal fresh flowers, or dried on a screen and then used in herbal wreaths. You can also use them in aromatic dried bouquets that are meant to serve as good luck talismans. At various times in history, charms laced with bay have been believed to ward off evil spirits, sickness, and even lightning.

Growing Your Own Bay

A long-lived woody shrub or small tree hardy to Zone 8 (see "Know Your Hardiness Zone" on page 85), bay makes a fine houseplant to keep indoors in winter, and then shift to a partially shaded spot outdoors in summer. In containers, bay usually grows 3 to 4 feet tall, although it can reach twice that size when grown outdoors in warm climates. Bay plants often survive temperatures as low as 20°F, although it's best to keep the temperature above 40°F at all times. Allow the soil in the container to become dry between waterings, and feed the plants monthly during the summer with a mix-with-water all-purpose plant food. Bay plants are usually slow growers and need repotting only every two to three years. Do not be alarmed if some of the old leaves drop off in late spring as new ones emerge at the stem tips. This is completely normal.

BORAGE

USES:	culinary, ornamental
BOTANICAL NAME:	*Borago officinalis*
OTHER COMMON NAMES:	bee bread
AREAS OF ORIGIN:	Europe, Western Asia, North Africa

According to myth, happiness and courage are symbolized by borage. This herb's crisp cucumber-like flavor and nodding blue flowers are certainly sufficient for gladdening the heart. If you want borage, you'll probably have to grow your own because it is seldom sold fresh and defies all methods of preservation (except in flavored vinegar). The good news is that borage is easy to grow. Among fans of edible flowers, borage blossoms are a treasured seasonal treat. Indeed, during the brief weeks in midsummer when borage is in bloom, you may find yourself indulging in the happiness they bring to every meal. Use the flowers to garnish drinks, salads, and cold summer soups.

Culinary Uses

Borage leaves have a distinct cucumber-like flavor, but it's important to use only those that are young and tender. Older leaves are often tough and extremely hairy. Even young leaves are a bit furry, although brief cooking turns them soft and succulent. Toss a few borage leaves into summer stir-fries or vegetable dishes in which they will wilt slightly from brief cooking. When using borage leaves raw, as you might when adding them to cold cucumber soup, chop them very finely, which will give them a more pleasing texture. It is best to cook with relatively small amounts of borage, because the leaves contain a compound that could be toxic to the liver if consumed in very large amounts. You can also use borage leaves to flavor vinegar (see "Making Herbal

Vinegars" on page 47). After the leaves are strained from the vinegar, place a sprig of borage flowers in the final product.

Fresh borage flowers make a beautiful garnish, or you can chop them into cheese spreads, sprinkle them in salads, or freeze them in ice cubes and add them to drinks. The notion that borage promotes courage can be traced back to Celtic warriors who drank borage-flavored wine before battle. A few borage blossoms added to a light white wine may give you similar effects.

Ornamental Uses

Borage plants grow to about 3 feet tall and feature a skirt of broad lower leaves, so they require a bit of room in the garden. One practical idea is to grow three borage plants together, arranged in a small clump or triangle, with smaller herbs nearby. Many gardeners believe that borage should be included in both vegetable gardens and strawberry patches, as it attracts bees and is thought to repel destructive insects.

Growing Your Own Borage

A fast-growing annual, borage needs full sun in cool climates, yet appreciates partial shade where summers are very hot. Sow seeds where you want the plants to grow as soon as days become warm in mid spring. Any deeply culti-vated soil will do provided it has a near neutral pH. (See "Checking the Soils pH" on page 88.) Thin seedlings to at least 12 inches apart. Bloom time is usu-ally midsummer. If plants are allowed to develop and shed mature seeds, vol-unteer seedlings often appear on their own in subsequent years. Borage can be grown in containers, where it makes a fine central upright plant to preside over smaller trailing herbs such as thyme or mints.

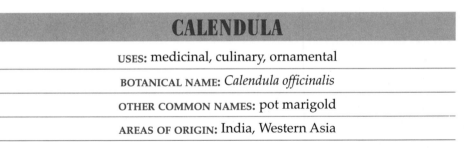

CALENDULA

USES:	medicinal, culinary, ornamental
BOTANICAL NAME:	*Calendula officinalis*
OTHER COMMON NAMES:	pot marigold
AREAS OF ORIGIN:	India, Western Asia

If you want to use your precious time, energy, and gardening space to grow only plants that have multiple purposes, calendula should not be missed. Dependable and easy to grow, calendulas are here and gone in a single season, but their yield of blossoms is always impressive. They make excellent cut flowers, and the petals can be used in cooking, too. Calendula's medicinal credentials are impressive as well. These are the flowers that Shakespeare refers to as "marybuds."

Medicinal Uses

MARIGOLD MIX-UPS
Don't confuse calendula with marigolds, which look similar. Only two marigold species are edible: gem or signet (*T. tenuifolia*), and Mexican tarragon (*T. lucida*). Both lack calendula's medicinal properties.

Monks in medieval monasteries grew calendula, which they brewed into strong tea and then used for cleaning wounds. Calendula petals contain antiseptic and anti-inflammatory properties, and preparing them for medicinal use is easy. Research has shown that some of this herb's active ingredients are water soluble, while others are fat soluble. To make the most of what calendula has to offer, be sure to dry some blossoms to always have on hand. Like the monks of times past, you can then brew the dried flowers into a strong tea, and use it to dab on skinned knees or other minor abrasions (after they have been cleansed with soap and water, of course). In addition, during the summer, when fresh blooms are abundant, make a double-infused oil to use as a skin ointment for rashes and scrapes or to aid recovery from sunburn. To make a double-infused oil, follow the instructions for making infused oil (see "Homemade Herbal Remedies for External Use" on page 35). After straining the infused oil, repeat the process with a second batch of fresh blossoms in the same oil. If you do not grow calendula yourself, you can purchase calendula creams and ointments at health food stores.

Culinary Uses

Calendula is often called "poor man's saffron" because the petals make such a fine substitute for saffron, which is quite expensive. Whether you use them fresh or dried, calendula petals add lively orange color to rice, pasta, potatoes, cakes, and muffins. The flavor of the fresh petals is slightly bitter, but the taste usually disappears in cooked dishes. Fresh petals tossed into a salad add nutrition in the form of lutein, a powerful antioxidant. You can also add petals to tea, where they add color and combine well with the flavors of mint and all of the lemon-scented herbs.

Ornamental Uses

Historically, the flowers of calendula are bright orange, and orange varieties are the best ones to grow if you are using them for medicinal or culinary purposes. In the garden, bright orange calendula flowers go well visually with herbs that bloom blue, such as borage and sage. Edging a bed of calendulas with blue or white pansies or lobelia is another eye-appealing recommendation. Blue bachelor buttons also make fine bed partners for calendulas, as they grow and bloom on a similar schedule and coordinate nicely in terms of color, size, and foliage texture. Full-sized calendula varieties grow to about 28 inches tall, while most dwarf varieties grow to only 12 inches.

Growing Your Own Calendula

Calendula is a cool-season annual, which means that you can sow seeds or set out seedlings very early in the spring. Seedlings grown in small containers are widely available in the spring in most areas. In semitropical climates, they are often sold in autumn for growing through the winter. Calendulas are easy to grow in any sunny, well-drained site, and soil fertility is always reflected in the size and vigor of the plants. To keep plenty of new flowers coming, snip off old blossoms once a week, or gather perfect blossoms for cooking or drying every few days. Blooming often falls off in very hot weather, though well-tended plants will make a strong comeback when cooler weather returns.

CARAWAY

USES: medicinal, culinary

BOTANICAL NAME: *Carum carvi*

OTHER COMMON NAMES: none

AREAS OF ORIGIN: Middle East, Central Europe

The classic seed of rye bread, caraway has been used in medicine and cooking for thousands of years. The edible plant parts are the oblong seeds, which are actually considered fruits. This is apparent if you sample their flavor in the Middle Eastern tradition, which involves candying them in sugar syrup and then munching on them at the end of a meal. An essential flavoring in German and Austrian cuisines, caraway seeds are thought to reduce the cooking odor of cabbage when added to the simmering water.

Medicinal Uses

Although caraway is seldom used medicinally, it may help settle upset stomachs when taken as a mild tea or steeped in warm milk. Crushing the hard-coated seeds first, or chopping them coarsely with a knife, helps release their beneficial compounds.

Culinary Uses

A little caraway goes a long way, so only 1 teaspoon of seeds is sufficient to flavor a four-serving batch of cabbage, cauliflower, carrots, or parsnips. Long cooking times can cause caraway's flavor to change from nutty-anise-dill-like to slightly bitter. For this reason, it's best to add the seeds during the last fifteen minutes of cooking time. When using caraway in breads, add some seeds to the dough when preparing the last rising, and sprinkle additional seeds onto the crust. Young caraway leaves can be chopped into salads, sandwiches, or soups, where their impart a mild, dill-like flavor. The fleshy roots of caraway are commonly prepared like parsnips.

Growing Your Own Caraway

Caraway is normally biennial, although a few strains will produce seeds in a single season from seeds planted in spring. However, like parsley and other biennial plants, caraway flowers best when established plants are exposed to several weeks of cold. Hardy to Zone 5 (see "Know Your Hardiness Zone" on page 85), this is a good herb to sow in late summer, in any sunny, well-drained site. Plant the seeds where you want the plants to grow, because caraway does not transplant well. Soaking the seeds for three days, and then drying them on paper towels for a few hours prior to planting, often improves germination to nearly 100 percent. In Zones 5 and 6, covering the plants with mulch during the winter will help protect the roots from freezing and thawing. Soon after the winter ends, mature plants will send up flowering stems topped with umbels (flat circular clusters) of small white flowers. Several weeks later, when the seeds begin to turn dark brown, harvest the seed-bearing stems and hang them to dry in paper bags or over a paper-lined tray. After the seeds are harvested, you can dig up the roots and try them as a cooked vegetable.

CATNIP

USES: medicinal, aromatic

BOTANICAL NAME: *Nepeta cataria*

OTHER COMMON NAMES: none

AREAS OF ORIGIN: Europe, Asia

It is certainly no secret that catnip is a feline favorite. Compounds in catnip leaves, called nepetalactones, elicit highly pleasurable responses in about two-thirds of all cats, including big cats like lions and leopards. They sniff the leaves, rub against them, roll on the plants, and seem terribly happy just to be near catnip. For humans, however, the response is not nearly as dramatic. Catnip tea may work as a very mild sedative, but claims that it is psychoactive are unfounded. In the garden, catnip has been found to repel several destructive insect pests, including aphids, Colorado potato beetles, and squash bugs.

Medicinal Uses

For many people, catnip tea has a calming effect. It can make a soothing night-cap, and even help induce sleep in certain individuals. Regardless of whether or not catnip tea has this particular effect on you, the magnesium and manganese it contains makes it a healthful beverage.

Aromatic Uses

There are two main ways to discover if your cat is attracted to catnip. Either buy a catnip toy and see if your feline friend responds to it, or try growing your own catnip plants. If you find your cat sniffing around the garden, rubbing and rolling around in the catnip, you can be sure the attraction is there. Keep in mind that not all cats have this pleasurable reaction, and although yours may not, don't be surprised if you find some of the neighborhood felines taking a liking to your plants. Interestingly, although it is beloved to some cats, the scent of catnip has no effect on other animals or people. It does, however, repel some insects, which is reason enough to welcome it into your herb garden.

Growing Your Own Catnip

A short-lived perennial hardy to Zone 4 (see "Know Your Hardiness Zone" on page 85), catnip can be grown from seed or from cuttings taken in spring from established plants. Some plants grow to 3 feet tall when they are in full flower, although those grown in partial shade will be shorter. The seeds of catnip are very small yet numerous. This herb now grows wild in many areas, and it will reseed itself in the garden with little help. Catnip leaves reach their maximum potency just after the plants begin to flower. Cut the stems to within 5 inches of the ground and dry by hanging them in small bunches. With adequate water, the plants should regrow enough leaves to take a second cutting in early autumn. Catnip plants often lose vigor after they are about three years old. To insure a constant supply, root stem cuttings in early spring or nurture seedlings found scattered in the garden. If neighborhood cats tend to destroy your planting, try growing catnip beneath a chicken-wire cage.

CATNIP'S FAMILY RELATIONS
Catmint (*Nepeta Faassenii*) is a popular hardy perennial grown for its spikes of blue flowers. Cats ignore catmint, as well as other *Nepeta* species, which are commonly grown as ornamentals.

CAYENNE PEPPER

USES: medicinal, culinary

BOTANICAL NAME: *Capsicum annuum*

OTHER COMMON NAMES: hot pepper, chili pepper

AREAS OF ORIGIN: Africa, Asia, Central America

Any pepper that tastes hot shares the talents of cayenne pepper, which is used here as a prime representative of all hot peppers. Hot peppers include such fiery favorites as jalapeños, habaneros, serranos, and many others. Their heat comes from chemical compounds called capsaicins. The concentration of capsaicin varies with the particular pepper varieties and the conditions under which they are grown. Hot weather makes any hot pepper hotter, while cool weather turns down the heat. Of all hot peppers, cayennes are the most popular because they are productive and easy to grow. They are also simple to dry and grind into flakes or powder.

The list of practical uses for hot peppers grows every day. You can use pepper spray to ward off mad dogs and muggers, sprinkle cayenne powder into your socks to help warm your feet, rub capsaicin cream on achy joints, or simply enjoy the way a little cayenne pepper adds depth and warmth to food. Hot pepper is widely used in pest control, too. Mammals from deer to squirrels are deterred by its taste.

Medicinal Uses

Cayenne pepper works by binding to the body's sensory receptors to heat. In addition to sending messages to the brain that register heat, the receptors can also block messages that the body is in pain. This two-punch effect explains how capsaicin soothes painful joints, warms cold hands and feet, and even numbs the pain of acute oral sores. However, capsaicin's pain relief comes at a price—an uncomfortable burning sensation. To use capsaicin, you must be careful to balance the burn with the benefit. This means starting out modestly, using only a little. And care must be taken that the capsaicin never comes in contact with eyes, mucous membranes, or open wounds.

Commercially made capsaicin creams and ointments for treating aches and pains are readily available. You can also make your own oil by steeping some hot peppers in warm vegetable oil for a few days. Whether the product is commercial or homemade, it's wise to wear disposable gloves when applying this herbal remedy. And if you find that the burning sensation on the treated area is too intense, wash off the cream or oil with some whole milk or sour cream. The fat in these dairy products is an effective capsaicin cleanser.

To use capsaicin to warm cold hands and feet, mix a small amount of cayenne pepper into any body powder, and sprinkle it into your socks or gloves. Again, it's important to begin with only a little, and increase the amount once you become aware of your personal tolerance levels.

As long as you do not have a stomach ulcer, you can use cayenne pepper (available in capsule form) to treat acute indigestion. In the stomach, cayenne pepper works just like it does on your skin, by interrupting pain signals being sent to your brain. And, although you might think that the last way to fight the fire of mouth sores would be with more fire, doctors have found that when cancer patients suffering from oral sores were given cayenne taffy to chew, they experienced pain relief that lasted for several hours. Using a mouthwash solution of 1 teaspoon cayenne mixed in a cup of water has a similiar effect.

Culinary Uses

Cayenne's culinary forms range from powders and flakes to whole dried peppers. Only a very small amount of cayenne is needed to add a spark of heat to foods; using more can increase the heat to four-alarm levels! As always, when

CAYENNE'S FAMILY RELATIONS

In addition to cayennes, you can grow other hot peppers in your garden, including super-hot habaneros and comparatively mild jalapeños. Pepper variety strongly influences its heat, which is rated in Scoville units—the higher the number, the hotter the pepper. Cayennes are typically rated at 55,000 units, jalapeños around 5,000, and some habaneros have been known to top 200,000 units—too hot for most people to handle.

PEPPERED BIRDSEED
Squirrels raiding your
bird feeder? Mixing
cayenne pepper with
the seeds will deter
them. Birds won't be
bothered because they
lack the receptors for
sensing capsaicin.

using cayenne or any other hot pepper to flavor food, begin with small amounts, then allow personal taste to guide you in adding more.

Pepper flakes and powder add both color and flavor to foods. Whole dried peppers, which are commonly used to turn up the heat in Oriental fare, are often removed from the dish just before serving. Marinating some hot peppers in vinegar for a few weeks will result in a simple pepper sauce, while puréeing hot peppers and vinegar together results in a thicker sauce that is extremely potent, especially when it is first made.

Growing Your Own Cayenne Peppers

Cayenne peppers are very easy to grow, as are other small-fruited peppers that have high concentrations of capsaicin. Peppers are warm-season annuals that cannot tolerate cold weather, so wait until late spring, when the soil is warm, to set out seedlings. You can grow seedlings yourself on a very sunny windowsill, or buy them at any garden center. Always grow peppers in full sun. To insure good pollination, grow at least two or three plants in the same plot. You can use cayenne peppers while they are still green, but wait until they turn red to gather them for drying. Cayennes are easy to dry because they have thin walls—many people thread string through the tops of the peppers and hang them in a warm room. Once the peppers are dry, store them whole in a glass jar or other airtight container, and keep in a cool, dark place.

CHAMOMILE

USES: medicinal, culinary, aromatic, ornamental

BOTANICAL NAME: *Matricaria recutita*

OTHER COMMON NAMES: German chamomile

AREA OF ORIGIN: Europe, Africa, Asia

One of the easiest herbs to grow, chamomile boasts an impressive list of practical uses, plus it looks and smells wonderful. The useful plant part is the blossom, a neat little daisy-like flower with white petals surrounding a round yellow center. Cultivated since the time of Hippocrates (377 B.C.), chamomile has a very respectable safety record. Even so, rare individuals who are allergic to ragweed also may have an allergic reaction to chamomile and should, therefore, avoid its use.

Medicinal Uses

Chamomile has a reputation as a natural sedative, and many herbal teas that are recommended for sipping before bedtime include chamomile. To make the most of this relaxing attribute, steep chamomile tea for at least ten minutes. However, because chamomile is a very mild relaxant no matter how strong the tea, you can enjoy a cup anytime without worrying that it will cause drowsiness.

THE OTHER CHAMOMILE
Roman chamomile produces flowers similar to those of German chamomile, with the same medicinal and aromatic qualities. It is easy to grow if you live in a cool maritime climate, but often fails in extreme winter cold or summer heat.

Lesser known but much more potent is chamomile's ability to soothe a nervous stomach and intestinal cramps. In addition to its anti-inflammatory and antimicrobial compounds, chamomile contains antispasmodics to calm a disturbed digestive tract. Steeping 2 teaspoons of dried flowers per cup of water for fifteen minutes results in a soothing tea to help settle intestinal troubles.

You also can use a strong chamomile tea as a mouthwash to help combat gingivitis and to aid in the healing of mouth sores. In addition, German research indicates that weak chamomile tea, cooled and filtered to remove small particles, makes a healing eyewash for irritated eyes.

Culinary Uses

A few fresh chamomile blossoms tossed into a salad make an eye-catching addition that impart a subtle floral flavor with a slightly bitter edge. They also make a decorative garnish for cold drinks. Because of their distinctly bitter flavor, stems and leaves should be removed before adding the flowers to foods or beverages.

Aromatic Uses

Crushed chamomile flowers release a refreshing green-apple-like scent, which is always strongest when the blossoms are fresh. For sheer sniffing pleasure, crush a few in your hands when you find them in the garden. To retain the aroma of chamomile flowers (which also reflects their medicinal potency), gather the little blossoms when they are in peak condition, and dry them in a slow oven, as is done with culinary herbs. (See page 45 for drying techniques) Store the dried blossoms in an airtight container, and keep in a cool, dark place. Many health food stores sell dried chamomile blossoms by the ounce. Before you buy, sniff the contents of the container to make sure the chamomile still has its distinctive green-apple aroma.

Ornamental Uses

A fast-growing annual with delicate, ferny foliage, chamomile plants grow to about 18 inches tall, and then cover themselves with hundreds of button-sized blossoms in early summer. Always pretty no matter where it is grown, chamomile is a good plant to naturalize in your garden or perhaps in a wild-flower meadow. If you allow a few plants to shed seeds, new seedlings will appear year after year in surprising places. Grow it once, and you will surely recognize the seedlings when they appear. Allow blossoms that are not harvested to mature on the plants until they begin to turn light brown and start to fall apart. Then, scatter the blossoms wherever you want plants to pop up next year.

Growing Your Own Chamomile

A classic summer annual, chamomile can be sown each spring by simply sprinkling the tiny seeds over the soil where you want the plants to grow. Pat the seeds gently to settle them in place, and begin looking for seedlings after two weeks. Should too many appear, thin the plants to 10 inches apart. Chamomile grows best in full sun, although it can handle partial shade in warm climates.

Expect plants to decline soon after they produce a bounteous crop of blossoms. In addition to encouraging plants to reseed themselves, you can gather a few dozen ripe blossoms for the little seeds they contain, and sow the seeds the following spring. You need not separate the seeds from the other flower parts. Simply collect some blossoms that are on the verge of turning brown on the plants, bring them indoors to dry for a few days, and then store them in an envelope or plastic bag until the following spring.

CHERVIL

USES: culinary

BOTANICAL NAME: *Anthriscus cerefolium*

OTHER COMMON NAMES: French parsley

AREAS OF ORIGIN: Europe, Asia

Like asparagus and strawberries, chervil ranks among the definitive flavors of spring. In the French tradition, chervil is combined with chives, parsley, and tarragon to make the seasoning *fines herbes*, but its flavor is distinctive enough to stand on its own. Chervil tastes best when grown in cool weather, which brings out a rich anise-parsley-like flavor that can become too strong when the plants are exposed to heat or drought. This is one culinary herb you will need to grow yourself if you want to sample it at its best—fresh from the garden—because fresh chervil is not available in most stores. And its flavor is too weak to come through in vinegars. When dried, chervil becomes tasteless.

Culinary Uses

Fresh chervil should be used raw or only *very* slightly cooked. A light sprinkling of this fresh herb with perhaps a dab of butter makes a wonderful addition to many steamed spring vegetables, including asparagus, peas, new potatoes, and baby carrots. Chervil also partners well with eggs, cheese, and noodle dishes, and fresh sprigs can be tossed into spring salads. Chervil's leaves and flowers make edible garnishes for salads, sandwiches, and cream soups.

Growing Your Own Chervil

A fast-growing annual herb with a strong preference for cool weather, chervil can be planted twice each year, in spring and again in autumn. Sow the seeds indoors and set out the little plants soon after they germinate, or simply plant the seeds where you want them to grow outdoors. In pots or in the garden, lightly press the seeds into prepared soil rather than covering them completely. You can begin picking outer leaves six weeks or so after planting. Chervil planted in spring usually produces white flowers, followed by seeds in early to midsummer. If allowed to mature, these seeds sometimes "self-sow," so that an autumn crop of volunteer seedlings appears when nights become cool in late summer.

CHIVES

USES: culinary, ornamental

BOTANICAL NAME: *Allium schoenoprasum*

OTHER COMMON NAMES: fine chives

AREA OF ORIGIN: China

People have kept chives in gardens for more than 5,000 years, and today this herb's popularity knows no geographical boundaries. The most delicately flavored members of the onion family, chives are extremely easy to grow. The plants feature beautiful flowers in addition to tasty leaves, which are produced over a very long season. Many people enjoy chives on baked potatoes, which is a lovely partnership but only the beginning of this herb's many uses in the kitchen. Chive flowers are as edible as are the plant's hollow leaves. You can also display this herb's lovely lilac-colored fresh blossoms in a vase.

Culinary Uses

The mild flavor of chives makes them acceptable to most palates when eaten raw, a claim that cannot be made for other members of the onion family. You can also add them to a dish as it finishes cooking, or use them as a garnish. For a beautiful presentation, use chives to tie long cylindrical vegetables such as asparagus, carrots, or green beans into small bundles before steaming. You can add chives to herb butters, mix them with cream cheese for a sandwich spread, or add them to omelets, cream sauces, or other dishes that are naturally mild flavored. You can snip chives into little pieces with kitchen scissors, or mince them on a cutting board with a sharp knife. Chives that are dried at home usually have very little flavor; the commercial versions, which are freeze-dried, are much more flavorful. To preserve chives at home, chop them and freeze in ice cube trays (see page 45).

Chive blossoms are a wonderful edible garnish, or you can break them up and use them the same way you use the chopped leaves. Beautiful in salads, chive blossoms are also very popular for use in herbal vinegar. Begin with a white vinegar (such as white rice vinegar), and the chive blossoms will give it a light rosy-pink tint. (See "Making Herbal Vinegars" on page 47.)

Ornamental Uses

The grassy texture of chive leaves make them a welcome addition to collections of herbs, particularly when you want to plant several perennials together in a single container. When in full bloom, a mature clump of chives is so pretty that you may be reluctant to gather the flowers. Yet removing the blossoms often prolongs the bloom time while encouraging plants to expend their energy producing new leaves. Chives are pretty enough to include in flower gardens, and they are believed to repel insect pests from roses and other plants.

Growing Your Own Chives

CHIVE'S FAMILY RELATIONS

Garlic chives are as hardy and vigorous as regular chives, and their flat leaves have a strong hint of garlic. They bloom in late summer, and have white blossoms that are so pretty, many gardeners grow them for the flowers alone.

A sun-loving perennial that is hardy to Zone 3 (see "Know Your Hardiness Zone" on page 85), chives ask only for regular water and reasonably fertile soil to be happy garden residents. When grown in containers (for which they are extremely well suited), chives benefit from feeding with a mix-with-water fertilizer every three weeks or so from spring until autumn. Chives can be grown from seed, but it's much faster to start with purchased plants or perhaps a small clump. Early spring is the best season to start a new planting, because chives are one of the first herbs to emerge from winter dormancy. They then grow a thick flush of leaves, followed by flowers in late spring. If you harvest leaves by popping off one or two long leaves per clump every few days, the plants will often continue to produce nonstop all summer and well into autumn. The plants die back when the freezing weather comes, but they need no special protection to insure their return in the spring. To keep plants vigorous and healthy, most people dig up and divide the clumps every three to four years, preferably in late winter or late summer after the flowers have faded.

CILANTRO/CORIANDER

USES: culinary

BOTANICAL NAME: *Coriandrum sativum*

OTHER COMMON NAMES: Chinese parsley

AREA OF ORIGIN: Eastern Mediterranean

Here is a culinary herb of worldwide popularity that is really two herbs in one. The leaves of young plants, which resemble flat-leafed parsley, are staples in Mexican, Chinese, and Thai cooking. When used in leaf form, this herb is properly called cilantro. After the plants flower and produce seeds, the round nutty fruits become a different spice—coriander. Coriander is an essential flavoring in curries and many other dishes of Indian origin. And although this herb's roots are rarely sold in stores, many gardeners, particularly in Southeast Asia, dig them up and use them. After they are scrubbed clean, the roots are chopped and then added to salty pickled condiments.

Culinary Uses

People who like the citrusy-savory flavor of cilantro leaves enjoy them raw, chopped into salsas and salads, or layered in sandwiches. When used in a cooked dish, cilantro should be added at the last minute to preserve its color and flavor. When dried, cilantro loses much of its flavor, so fresh is always recommended. Sold in bunches and found in the produce section of most supermarkets, cilantro, like parsley, will keep in the refrigerator for several days.

You can also freeze the fresh leafy stems after they have been rinsed and patted dry. (See page 44 for freezing techniques.)

Coriander is sold as whole seed or ground into a powder. Opt for the whole seeds, which keep their flavor for more than a year. Before using, roast the seeds in a dry skillet over low heat for a few minutes, or until you can smell their nutty aroma. Allow them to cool, and then coarsely grind or chop with a heavy knife. A few crushed coriander seeds make a welcome addition to any curry dish, and they are an ideal flavor accent for lentils, rice, mushrooms, tomatoes, and many other vegetables.

Growing Your Own Cilantro/Coriander

A fast-growing annual, cilantro grows best in cool weather. When sown in autumn, established plants often survive winter in Zones 7 and 8 (see "Know Your Hardiness Zone" on page 85). Elsewhere, sow seeds where you want the plants to grow first thing in spring, and again in late summer for an autumn crop. Choose a sunny spot, and use very little fertilizer, which can make the leaves taste bland.

Cilantro seeds germinate in only a few days if they are soaked overnight in water, and planted in the soil about a half inch deep. If too many seedlings appear, thin the plants to about 5 inches apart. As you need cilantro in the kitchen, begin picking individual leaves when the plants are about six weeks old. Soon thereafter, the shape of the leaves will become very thin and feathery as the plants suddenly grow taller and prepare to flower. If you also want to harvest coriander seeds, allow the plants to mature completely, and cut the seed-bearing stems when about half of the seeds have changed from green to grayish-tan. Hang the stems indoors in paper bags for a couple of weeks. When completely dry, the seeds will fall easily from the stems. Pick through the seeds by hand, removing and discarding any foreign material, and then store in airtight glass jars.

THE BEDBUG HERB
Coriander plants are chameleon-like in aroma. Young leafy plants bear the savory scent of cilantro. At the flowering and fruitset stage, they give off a slightly acrid smell that is similar to the odor emitted by the bedbug. But don't worry. The scent is short-lived and hardly noticeable in the garden.

COMFREY

USES: medicinal, ornamental

BOTANICAL NAME: *Symphytum officinale*

OTHER COMMON NAMES: knitbone

AREAS OF ORIGIN: Europe, Asia

Used as a medicinal herb since at least 400 B.C., comfrey is a rich source of allantoin, a protein that stimulates cell growth. Poultices that were made from the leaves and applied to sprains and broken bones earned comfrey the name knitbone. Today, comfrey is still valued in the treatment of many skin problems and sprains, and it is especially useful when improved circulation contributes to the cure. Although comfrey teas and infusions were once widely used to treat colds and bronchitis, this herb is now known to contain compounds that are toxic to the liver and may cause cancer. In recent years, comfrey products for internal use have been banned in the United States, Great Britain, Canada, and Germany.

Medicinal Uses

When used appropriately, which means applying preparations to sprains, bruises, persistent skin problems (such as psoriasis or eczema), or slow-healing leg or foot ulcers no more than four times a day, comfrey has a strong track record of promoting healing. Comfrey works by stimulating cell growth and increasing the ability of skin cells to hold water. You can make your own comfrey compress by using either the plant's roots or fresh young leaves, but many people prefer to err on the side of safety by using commercial creams or ointments from which the pyrrolizidine alkaloids, the compounds known to cause liver damage, have been removed. These products are widely available at health food stores and herb shops.

Ornamental Uses

Comfrey is a large plant, often growing 4 feet tall and equally wide. Grown as an ornamental plant, comfrey forms a large, lush mound that is topped by spires of nodding blue flowers. Its large leaves shade the surrounding soil, smothering weeds and helping to keep the soil moist. This herb thrives in partial shade, where it usually blooms in early to midsummer, and then persists well into autumn. It is so vigorous that many gardeners pull off the leaves and use them to mulch the ground around other plants. In the landscape, comfrey is a wonderful plant to grow at the base of a fence or to position behind variegated hostas or ferns as a dark green backdrop in the shade garden.

Growing Your Own Comfrey

A vigorous perennial hardy to Zone 3 (see "Know Your Hardiness Zone" on page 85), comfrey emerges in early spring, grows all summer, and then dies back to the ground in late autumn. You can grow comfrey from seeds or plant a piece of dormant root in early spring. Comfrey likes a rich, moist soil with a pH that is neutral or slightly alkaline. (See "Checking the Soil's pH" on page 88.) Once established, comfrey persists for years, and it is often necessary to dig out plants if the colony becomes too large.

DILL

USES: culinary, ornamental

BOTANICAL NAME: *Anethum graveolens*

OTHER COMMON NAMES: dillweed

AREA OF ORIGIN: Central Europe

In Colonial America, branches of dill were believed to repel witches. But eventually, superstition gave way to good eating. The thin, threadlike leaves of dill are often called dillweed, although there is nothing weedy about this beautiful plant. After producing round flat-topped clusters of yellow flowers, the plants bear flavorful seeds, which are used to flavor pickles, fish, and many other dishes.

Culinary Uses

Dill leaves carry a delicate hint of anise with a sweet, savory aftertaste, especially when they are fresh and juicy. The finely chopped leaves work well with many dairy-based dips and sauces. You also can chop the leaves into salads, add them to pasta or noodles just before serving, or use them as a colorful flavor accent for root vegetables, squash, fish, or even apples. Dilled butter is excellent on hot crusty bread, and cheese spreads spiked with dill can turn ordinary sandwiches into taste sensations. For the best flavor, use fresh dill leaves or ones that have been frozen. Dried dill weed is widely sold on spice shelves, but its flavor is extremely weak.

Unlike its leaves, dill's seeds do not suffer in storage. The primary flavoring used in dill pickles, dill seeds are commonly added to vinegar-based marinades for many vegetables, including beets, summer squash, and green beans. Dill bread makes use of dill seeds as well, and many salty fish dishes from Northern Europe are accented with dill seeds.

Ornamental Uses

In the garden, feathery dill foliage often has a blue-green hue. The plant's combination of soft texture and cooling color make it a fine choice to partner with bold yellow flowers. Dill also can be grown in containers in the company of other herbs. Many varieties grow to 4 feet tall, but there are some petite varieties, such as 'Fernleaf' dill, that grow to only 18 inches.

Growing Your Own Dill

SNIP IT
Many cooks snip dill using a small pair of kitchen scissors rather than chopping it with a knife, which tends to crush the delicate leaves.

A fast-growing annual, dill is best planted from seed in a sunny, well-drained spot in the garden in spring, as soon as the last frost has passed. If you buy plants, handle them gently and disturb the roots as little as possible as you set them out. Three plants, arranged in a group so that each plant is 12 inches from its nearest neighbor, will form a large mound of feathery foliage and produce plenty of leaves and seeds. To harvest the seeds, wait until several weeks after the yellow flowers have faded, and the seeds on the outside of each cluster begin to turn brown. Carefully cut the seed-bearing stems and hang them to dry in paper bags or over sheets of newspaper. Pick through the seeds by hand, removing and discarding any foreign material, and then store in airtight glass jars.

ECHINACEA

USES:medicinal, ornamental

BOTANICAL NAME:*Echinacea angustifolia, E. pallida, E. purpurea*

OTHER COMMON NAMES:coneflower, purple coneflower

AREA OF ORIGIN:Central North America

More people buy echinacea products than any other medicinal herb, and it is also a popular perennial flower to grow in a sunny garden. The plant that gardeners call purple coneflower (*E. purpurea*) is the type of echinacea most commonly used for medicinal purposes. Native American tribes of the Great Plains used the three closely related species of echinacea named here to treat illnesses ranging from cancer to snakebite. All three are medicinally active. Today, scientific studies have shown that echinacea is effective in helping to fight off colds.

Can you have echinacea to use as a home remedy and enjoy the beautiful flowers, too? Yes, but doing so takes patience and planning. Medicinally, the most potent plant part is the root, and the prettiest plants, classified as *Echinacea purpurea*, need at least two years, and usually three, to grow plump roots that are suitable for harvesting. And echinaceas bloom best when they are left undisturbed, so there is a dilemma here. Fortunately, the roots of a single mature plant, dug in late autumn after the tops have died back and the plant has become dormant, will provide ample material for a sizeable batch of tincture. So, by maintaining a permanent bed of echinacea, you should have no problem growing the flowers that are much loved by bees (and look great in a vase), and still be able to make use of the plant's medicinal riches.

Medicinal Uses

When taken at the first sign of any illness, and especially when you have been exposed to a cold, echinacea boosts the activity of your immune system. It increases the number of white blood cells (which attack bacteria and viruses), while inhibiting the ability of viruses and bacteria to reproduce. If, however, you still get the cold, there's a good chance that it won't be as severe or last as long with the help of echinacea. For maximum effectiveness, you should take echinacea three times a day, either as tea, liquid extract, or in 300 milligram capsules. More potent preparations are available, in which case you should follow label directions.

There is some controversy (and no scientific answers) regarding whether it is better to take echinacea on an ongoing basis, or only when you feel that you are at high risk for getting sick. The rationale for taking echinacea on an as-needed basis is that your immune system should be allowed to follow its natural cycles of action, rest, and recovery, rather than being forced to stay on high alert all the time. Since echinacea is an immune-system stimulant, those who are pregnant or suffer from an autoimmune disorder such as lupus, multiple sclerosis, or rheumatoid arthritis, should take it only under specific instructions from their health care provider.

Commercially produced echinacea products are often made from all three species of echinacea, although none is necessarily superior for medicinal purposes. The best way to prepare echinacea for medicinal use at home is to make an alcohol-based tincture (see "Making Liquid Extracts" on page 32) from well-scrubbed, finely chopped roots. Glycerin tincture is a good second choice, especially if you plan to give the extract to children. The classic test for checking the potency of homemade extracts is to place several drops directly on your tongue. A slight tingling sensation indicates the presence of alkamides, a reliable sign that the plant's active components have been captured in the extract.

Ornamental Uses

Most home gardeners prefer purple coneflower (*E. purpurea*) because it has the largest and prettiest flowers. The 3-foot-tall plants are somewhat coarse of texture, and pair well with bedfellows that have soft, airy foliage, such as artemisia or yarrow. Bees are naturally drawn to the large pincushion-like cone in the middle of each blossom, and goldfinches and other small birds eagerly gather the ripe seeds. The ancestral color of all types of echinacea is a dusty mauve-pink, although white- and orange-flowered varieties are available. Pale coneflower (*E. pallida*) has very thin, backswept light pink petals.

Growing Your Own Echinacea

A cold-hardy, long-lived perennial at home in Zones 3 to 8 (see "Know Your Hardiness Zone" on page 85), echinacea grows best in cool climates with full sun, yet benefits from partial shade where summers are long and hot. Add a little lime to naturally acidic soil, because this flower prefers a near neutral soil pH. (See "Checking the Soil's pH" on page 88.) You can start plants from seed, but they will not bloom until their second year. It is faster to begin with container-grown plants, set out just as they are emerging from dormancy in early spring. Once established, echinaceas are quite tough, and they rarely have serious problems with pests or disease.

ELECAMPANE

USES: medicinal, ornamental

BOTANICAL NAME: *Inula helenium*

OTHER COMMON NAMES: wild sunflower, horse-heal

AREAS OF ORIGIN: Europe, Asia

Most herbs are small plants, but not this one. Elecampane usually grows 5 to 6 feet tall. Its size combined with lots of shaggy bright yellow blossoms makes it a sure-fire eye-catcher in the garden. Historically, elecampane has been a medicinal herb, and it is still used to treat coughs, bronchitis, and other pulmonary problems. This herb's name (as well as its botanical name) can be traced to various legends involving Helen of Troy, popularized by Homer and other Greek writers as the fairest woman in the world. Loosely translated, Helena de la campagne (elecampane) means "Helen of the fields."

Medicinal Uses

Elecampane roots yield a very bitter tea that can be made palatable only by the addition of plenty of lemon, sugar, or honey. In Russia, the solution to elecampane's flavor problem is to mix a liquid extract made from the root with a jigger of vodka; a swig of strong-flavored juice or lemonade makes a good substitute. At health food stores, you can also find elecampane in tablet form. Regardless of its form, elecampane is usually taken three times a day for the treatment of lung or bronchial congestion. And, although it is often listed as a preferred herbal treatment for coughing children, its taste must be masked before kids find it acceptable. If you cannot find an elecampane syrup made for children, mix 10 drops of extract into 1 tablespoon of juice concentrate.

You can also make elecampane tea from the roots of homegrown plants. To prepare the roots, scrub them well and then remove any corky or woody sections with a sharp knife. Then cut the roots into shreds before drying them in a warm oven. When dry almost to the point of crispness, store the shredded root in airtight jars. Use the dried root to make a tea that is steeped for at least fifteen minutes, or to make liquid extract (see "Making Liquid Extracts" on page 32).

Ornamental Uses

Tall and shaggy with bristly leaves and stems, elecampane occasionally grows to 8 feet tall in very hospitable sites. Because of its size, elecampane is a striking background plant for the garden. Either full sun or partial shade will please this giant daisy-like plant, which is actually a cousin to asters. Elecampane plants usually do not reach their maximum size until they are two to three years old.

Growing Your Own Elecampane

Elecampane is a tough, long-lived perennial, hardy to Zone 3 (see "Know Your Hardiness Zone" on page 85). If you start with seeds, sow them indoors in late winter, and set out the plants in mid spring. You can also begin with a piece of dormant root or a purchased plant. Elecampane appreciates moist soil, so it is a good plant for low, wet places. Once established, the plants grow into clumps, which can be dug up and divided as roots are harvested. The best time to harvest roots for medicinal purposes is in autumn. The roots of two-year-old plants are often of the best quality, though woody roots of older plants may be harvested as well.

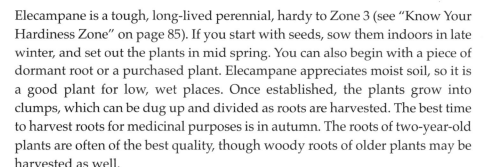

FENNEL

USES: medicinal, culinary, ornamental

BOTANICAL NAME: *Foeniculum vulgare*

OTHER COMMON NAMES: common fennel

AREA OF ORIGIN: Middle East

Fennel is one of the oldest herbs in cultivation and also one of the most famous. Its agreeable flavor and ease of culture made it one of the first herbs to be shared between the Persians and the Greeks, who believed it increased strength while keeping one lean. Indeed, people trying to lose weight have long drunk fennel tea or eaten the stalks prior to meals to help control their appetites. This property has never been verified scientifically, but it may be more than a coincidence that fennel has helped people lose weight. In the culinary traditions of Greece, Italy, and France, fennel is often paired with grilled or poached fish, a staple dish in many modern weight-loss plans.

Medicinal Uses

Fennel teas and infusions were used to treat many illnesses during the Middle Ages, but today, this herb's medicinal uses are limited to treating minor indigestion and coughs due to colds. A mild tea, made from 1 teaspoon of seeds steeped in boiling water for ten minutes, is the usual preparation. Phytoestrogens (natural estrogen-like compounds found in plants) in fennel tea may foster a feeling of well-being in menopausal women, but for this reason, it should not be taken if you are pregnant. However, there are no known dangers associated with the small amounts of fennel used in cooking.

Culinary Uses

All parts of the fennel plant are edible. You can chop the tender young leaves into salads or cheese spreads, add them to egg dishes, or sprinkle them on baked fish or other meats. Dried fennel foliage has little flavor, but you can freeze the leaves in small containers. The stems tend to be a bit stringy, but they still make an interesting raw snack. Fennel seeds are essential ingredients in many English, Italian, and Polish sausages, and they are delicious on breadsticks, too. Lightly roasted and then crushed, fennel seeds make a nice flavor accent for cabbage, beets, potatoes, or beans.

Ornamental Uses

The light, airy foliage of fennel is almost cloudlike in its presence in the garden. Most varieties produce green foliage, and grow to about 4 feet tall when in full flower. There are also some varieties with bronze foliage that are popular for both herb gardens and flowerbeds. In either color, fennel plants produce extra stems that make lovely additions to cut flower arrangements.

Growing Your Own Fennel

Fennel is a perennial plant, but because it is hardy only to Zone 6 (see "Know Your Hardiness Zone" on page 85), it is often grown as an annual. Sow seeds in spring, in any sunny, well-drained spot. Work a moderate amount of slow-release all-purpose fertilizer into the soil before planting, because fennel will be scrawny if it is underfed. Begin picking leaves as you need them in the kitchen anytime. Expect to see round, flat-topped clusters of yellow flowers in midsummer, followed by fat grooved seeds. To harvest the seeds, cut the stems when the seeds begin to dry to brown, and hang them to dry in paper bags or over paper-lined trays. After two weeks, the seeds should be ready to shake loose, sort, and store in airtight glass jars. In areas where fennel is perennial, it is best to prune the plants back in late autumn, so that a mass of dead foliage does not smother the plants' crowns.

FENNEL'S FAMILY RELATIONS

Vegetable fennel (finocchio or Florence fennel) has a fat bulb of thick celery-like stems that are eaten raw or cooked. Its lacy leaves can be used in place of herb fennel in most recipes.

FEVERFEW

USES: medicinal, ornamental

BOTANICAL NAME: *Chrysanthemum parthenium*

OTHER COMMON NAMES: featherfew, wild chamomile

AREA OF ORIGIN: Central Europe

For hundreds of years, feverfew has been used for purposes ranging from treating dog bites to repelling fleas, so it is difficult to separate feverfew folk-lore from fact. One obvious truth about feverfew is that is a very pretty flower, deserving of space in any sunny garden. Another is that feverfew leaves, taken regularly, can reduce the frequency and severity of migraine headaches. Fever-few leaves are powerhouses of potent compounds, including natural blood thinners, so this is not an herb to take if you are pregnant or if you are expecting to undergo surgery.

Medicinal Uses

When taken internally, and especially on a daily basis, feverfew regulates the dilation of small blood vessels along with the spasms that are a frequent cause of migraine headaches. In addition, it reduces inflammation associated with arthritis. Feverfew is definitely a preventative type of medicine, but taking it daily can be challenging. The useful plant part is the leaf, and it's important to take the whole leaf or a whole-leaf extract. Unfortunately, the leaves taste bitter and it is not uncommon for them to cause mouth sores in susceptible individuals. The easiest way to take feverfew is to buy it in capsule form, but be sure to look for "standardized dose" on the product label. With feverfew, the standardized dose is 250 milligrams per day. For migraine prevention, it often takes several weeks of feverfew therapy to see noticeable improvement.

If you grow your own feverfew, preserve its properties for off-season use by making an alcohol-based liquid extract (see "Making Liquid Extracts" on page 32). In addition, during summer, when long-term storage is not an issue, finely chop some leaves and barely cover them with honey. Take 1 teaspoon of this mixture daily, either as is or spread on a small piece of bread.

MOSQUITO-FEW, TOO
Feverfew may discourage unwanted pests in your garden, as well as stinging or biting bugs. If you want to try feverfew as an insect repellent, make a very strong tea with fresh leaves, stems, and flowers, and splash it on both skin and dark-colored clothing.

Ornamental Uses

Perhaps the daintiest member of the chrysanthemum family, feverfew features clusters of button-sized daisy-like flowers, with white petals surrounding a yellow center. In containers, you can use a single plant as the central upright element, perhaps surrounded by sprawling mints or creeping thymes. In the garden, feverfew asks only for plenty of sun. Its close presence may help confuse aphids in search of your roses. Stems of feverfew make versatile and long-lasting cut flowers. Heavy-blooming varieties, including 'Snowball' and 'White Pompom,' have double flowers (which have twice as many white petals as regular feverfew). But compared with regular feverfew, the leaves of these varieties contain less parthenolide, the medicinally active ingredient.

Growing Your Own Feverfew

A tough perennial hardy to Zone 4 (see "Know Your Hardiness Zone" on page 85), feverfew is easy to grow and sometimes becomes slightly weedy as volunteer seedlings appear in unexpected places. These are easily controlled by simply pulling them out. Individual plants seldom grow taller than 24 inches, and may be half that height in poor soil. The biggest bloom comes in midsummer in most climates. The best time to harvest feverfew's leaves for medicinal use is early summer, just as blossom buds begin to form. After the flowers fade, cut back plants by one-third their size, and spoil them for a few weeks by feeding them every ten days with a mix-with-water fertilizer. When well pleased, feverfew often blooms a second time in autumn before becoming dormant in early winter. To shelter the shallow roots from winter damage, it is helpful to leave the dead aboveground plant parts intact through the winter. Then clip them off first thing in the spring.

GARLIC
USES: medicinal, culinary, aromatic
BOTANICAL NAME: *Allium sativum*
OTHER COMMON NAMES: none
AREA OF ORIGIN: Western Asia

Garlic has been used in food and medicines since before recorded history, and both of these uses continue today. As a spice, garlic is an essential ingredient in many of the most famous dishes in the world, from Italian pesto to Asian soups and dipping sauces. Medicinally, garlic is rich with compounds that thin the blood, thus regulating blood pressure. It also contains properties that fight bacterial, fungal, and viral infections. It is, therefore, no wonder that garlic is historically associated with strength and endurance. Paradoxically, the main limiting factor in using garlic to cure various ills—its pungent fragrance—is also its most endearing characteristic in the kitchen.

Medicinal Uses

If you want to use garlic to improve your health, the best way is by ingesting at least one clove a day. You might eat a little more if you have an infection that requires the use of antibiotics, because garlic may boost the effects of antibiotic drugs. The sulfur compounds in garlic are the secret to its antiviral properties, so fresh garlic is best if you feel like you're coming down with a cold. Currently, there is no solid evidence that encapsulated garlic or garlic oil has the same effects as ingesting fresh cloves, which is not bad news if you enjoy its flavor. Fortunately, ways to prepare garlic number in the thousands, and entire cookbooks are devoted to this beloved herb.

Culinary Uses

Garlic is sold in bulbs, each of which is comprised of a cluster of cloves. Most recipes call for a certain number of garlic cloves, which may be chopped or crushed after the papery peeling is removed. Uncooked garlic is extremely pungent and strong of flavor, but cooking makes garlic much more savory and brings out slight nutty highlights in its flavor. When cooking with garlic, take care it is not allowed to burn, which can happen quickly when it is being sautéed in oil. Burned garlic has a bitter taste. Also use restraint when adding raw garlic to herb butter or pesto. It is always best to add it a few hours before the food will be eaten, because raw garlic can become bitter when combined with other ingredients and left to ripen for too long. This is not a problem in dishes in which the garlic is cooked, even for a few seconds.

Aromatic Uses

The same substances that give people garlic breath can deter feeding by garden insects. Many gardeners find that a spray made from infusing five or more crushed cloves of garlic in a pint of water for several days repels insects from many flowers and vegetables. To help the spray stick to plant leaves, add a few drops of dishwashing soap to the garlic water after you have removed the crushed cloves and are ready to spray. To give this spray extra punch, add a few hot peppers to the infusion.

Growing Your Own Garlic

Hardy to Zone 5 (see "Know Your Hardiness Zone" on page 85), garlic grows on an unusual schedule. Cloves are planted in late autumn, pointed side up and about 4 inches deep in fertile, sun-drenched soil. Sometimes green shoots appear during the winter, but garlic's main task during winter months is to grow roots. The first tops that appear in spring are edible when very young and taste like garlicky green onions. But for the biggest bulbs, leave the tops uncut and let the plants grow until they begin to yellow, which can be early, mid, or late summer, depending on climate. Then dig up the bulbs, shake off the dirt, and allow them to dry in a warm, airy place for a few weeks. Once cured, garlic will store for months at room temperature.

There are several types of garlic, and one key to garlic-growing success is to choose the best type for your climate. Gilroy, California, is considered the garlic capital of North America, but garlic is grown commercially in other areas, too. If you can find out which strains are local favorites in your area, you can produce better quality garlic in your own backyard. For example, rocambole garlics, which are often streaked with red, usually do well in cold climates. Artichoke types of garlic produce larger bulbs that are usually white, and they grow best where winters are mild.

GINGER

USES: medicinal, culinary
BOTANICAL NAME: *Zingiber officinale*
OTHER COMMON NAMES: none
AREAS OF ORIGIN: India, China

Made from the fleshy roots of a tropical plant that looks like a cross between sugar cane and bamboo, ginger deserves much wider use, both medically and in cooking. In recent studies, ginger has been found to be as effective controlling nausea and arthritis pain as several leading prescription drugs. And while foods made with ginger taste wonderful, there may be excellent reasons why they also leave you with a glowing feeling of well-being. Ginger contains more than forty antioxidants, making it perhaps the most health-enhancing herb known to humankind. Unfortunately, because ginger cannot tolerate cold temperatures, it's not a good choice for home gardens.

Medicinal Uses

The list of conditions that may respond to ginger interventions is a long one, and includes nausea due to motion sickness, postoperative nausea, and morning sickness (see "Ginger for Morning Sickness" on page 155). Try one 250-milligram capsule or its equivalent ($\frac{1}{4}$ teaspoon freshly grated ginger or

1/8 teaspoon powder), at least a half hour before you expect to be exposed to motion sickness. If you're heading out to sea, take a bottle of candied ginger with you for munching. Sweetened ginger tea, which tastes great hot or cold, is also a delicious way to treat nausea. Many commercial ginger ales contain only a little ginger, but ginger spritzers sold at health food stores often pack a therapeutic dose.

Zingibain, an enzyme in ginger, is probably the power behind this herb's ability to reduce inflammation due to arthritis and rheumatism. Treat flare-ups with 1 teaspoon of fresh ginger, or two 250-milligram capsules, taken three times a day with meals. Other ways to take ginger include chewing the candied form, sipping tea that has been steeped with slices of gingerroot, and enjoying the pickled version. Beneficial compounds in ginger called sesquiterpenes have strong antiviral properties, which could be one reason why chicken soup spiked with plenty of ginger is a standard Chinese folk remedy for the common cold.

Culinary Uses

What would fried rice, Thai noodles, or most other Asian-inspired dishes be without the flavor of ginger? But this herb's unique essence is welcome in many non-Asian dishes as well. Ginger breads, cakes, and cookies are good examples; and the taste of many winter vegetables, such as acorn squash, sweet potatoes, and carrots, is commonly enhanced by ginger's flavorful spark. I keep four forms of ginger in my kitchen—ginger powder for baking, pickled ginger to enjoy as an edible garnish, candied ginger for adding to teas or eating straight out of the bottle, and of course the fresh root. There is no need to let leftover pieces of gingerroot turn green inside a plastic bag in your refrigerator. Instead, use a very sharp knife to cut the root into thin slices and freeze them in a small plastic container. The frozen slices break apart easily, and chopping them up is so fast and clean that you may prefer using frozen

GINGER FOR MORNING SICKNESS
One study found that ginger capsules reduced morning sickness during the first trimester of pregnancy—with no side effects. With your doctor's permission, try sipping a cup of ginger tea or swallowing a 1/4 teaspoon of grated ginger for morning sickness relief.

SMART SHOPPING
The best-quality ginger comes from tropical climates. Look for plump, smooth roots that are less than 2 inches in diameter in the produce section. Very large roots are often stringy inside.

ginger over the fresh root. Incidentally, as long as gingerroot is well cleaned with a thorough scrub under warm running water, there's no need to remove the skin unless you want to. The skin is every bit as edible as the inner flesh.

GINKGO

USES: medicinal, ornamental	
BOTANICAL NAME: *Ginkgo biloba*	
OTHER COMMON NAMES: maidenhair tree	
AREA OF ORIGIN: China	

Ginkgo has been around for 150 to 200 million years, and is touted as the oldest living tree species. It was considered a sacred herb in ancient China, and maintained for centuries by the monks there. Eventually, ginkgo made its way to Europe in the eighteenth century, where its medicinal properties promoted its use as a widely prescribed drug. The extract derived from the plant's fan-like leaves has been used primarily to enhance circulation. In addition to its medicinal benefits, ginkgo is grown throughout the world for its beauty. A ginkgo tree can be a beautiful addition to the landscape, particularly in autumn, when its leaves turn golden yellow just before fluttering to the ground.

Medicinal Uses

Hundreds of scientific studies have offered clinical evidence of ginkgo's effectiveness in increasing blood flow. Because of this positive effect on the vascular system, ginkgo has been useful in improving circulation in the extremities, relieving cold hands and feet, and in treating conditions such as vertigo, tinnitus, and sexual dysfunction. Ginkgo has also gained recognition as a kind of brain tonic that enhances memory, concentration, and mental clarity. It is often used to treat those with Alzheimer's disease. This herb's active ingredients have also been shown to control inflammation due to allergies, anaphylactic shock, and asthma, as well as relieve tension and anxiety, elevate mood, and restore energy, particularly in the elderly. Studies have found that ginkgo offers few benefits to young, healthy adults.

The therapeutic dose begins at 60 milligrams of ginkgo extract, taken twice a day, and may be raised to 240 milligrams daily if no side effects (such as stomach upset or abdominal cramping) are present. Ginkgo use should be discontinued prior to surgery since it has blood-thinning effects, and thus can lead to excessive bleeding. Because ginkgo must be highly concentrated, it is not practical to make preparations from this herb yourself.

Ornamental Uses

A slow-growing hardwood tree, ginkgo is most outstanding in autumn, when its leaves turn buttery gold all at once during mid to late season. An ideal tree for planting in an open lawn, young ginkgo trees slowly outgrow their awkward shapes and become symmetrical-spreading beauties by the time they are twenty years old.

Growing Your Own Ginkgo

Hardy to Zones 3 to 9 (see "Know Your Hardiness Zone" on page 85), ginkgo prefers full sun but can adapt to almost any type of soil. At maturity, ginkgo can be 50 feet tall and 30 feet wide. Ginkgo is dioecious, which means that some trees are male and others are female. The fruits produced by female trees emit a terrible odor, so nurseries sell mostly male clones, which do not present this problem. Set out container-grown trees in early spring, just before they emerge from winter dormancy. Ginkgo trees require no pruning and seldom have problems with pests and diseases.

SMART SHOPPING
All ginkgo supplements are not alike, so it is important to shop for products that offer a standardized dose of at least 60 milligrams. Tablets and capsules are the most popular way to take ginkgo.

GINSENG

USES:	medicinal
BOTANICAL NAME:	*Panax ginseng, P. quinquefolius*
OTHER COMMON NAMES:	seng
AREAS OF ORIGIN:	China, North America

The most revered herb in Chinese medicine, ginseng is not used to treat specific illnesses. Rather, it is considered an adaptogen, which is a substance that helps the body adapt to various types of stress in a balanced yet positive way. The word "tonic" could be used to describe ginseng, although this may understate its deeper value, which is to restore harmony to the body, resulting in enhanced energy. Both of the major species of ginseng are slow-growing woodland plants, one native to China (*P. ginseng*) and one native to the Eastern United States (*P. quinquefolius*).

Medicinal Uses

Scientific studies of ginseng's benefits have yielded mixed results; however, there is a noteworthy trend. When the experimental subjects are young, healthy, and vigorous there is often little difference reported in energy and overall well-being from taking ginseng. However, older people and those recovering from illness or other seriously stressful situations notice more dramatic results. Some people with diabetes find that ginseng lowers their blood sugar levels; therefore, it is essential that people with diabetes who take ginseng closely monitor their blood sugar levels.

For people who do not suffer from chronic diseases, perhaps the best use of ginseng is to increase alertness and mental acuity while promoting a feeling of calmness and serenity at the same time. Long road trips, intense work assignments, or dramatic personal crises may be easier to manage with the help of this herb.

Ginseng's most potent plant part is the root, which is dried before being packaged into teas, brewed into extracts, or powdered and packed into tablets or capsules. From the time a new plant sprouts from a seed, it takes at least five years (and often much longer) to produce a root of harvestable size. This explains why the purest medicinal forms of ginseng are quite expensive. However, because the active ingredients, called ginsenosides, are water soluble, teas labeled for standardized content are often a good way to take ginseng when you need it.

Because of its high cost, ginseng is often mixed with other ingredients in commercial preparations. The only way to be certain of a product's usefulness is to study the label to see if it offers a standardized dose of ginsenosides, and then follow label instructions. As you might expect, the more potent the product, the more expensive it is.

Growing Your Own Ginseng

Hardy to Zone 5 (see "Know Your Hardiness Zone" on page 85), ginseng requires a specific ecological niche: open woods with rich, humusy soil and about 70 percent shade, preferably on a north-facing slope. Each autumn, the plants produce a small cluster of red berries, which contain seeds. Knowledgeable collectors observe the Native American practice of bending this seedhead over, so the plants can develop fully mature seeds, before going back a few weeks later to dig up roots. This procedure insures that seeds are left behind and will grow into new plants. Never dig up roots from public land (or from private land without the owner's permission). Instead, either establish a bed or two as long-term garden projects, or buy ginseng in ready-to-use form. Because ginseng is an endangered plant, many states require certification that the roots are at least five years old before they can be sold.

GOLDENSEAL

USES:medicinal

BOTANICAL NAME:*Hydrastis canadensis*

OTHER COMMON NAMES:yellow puccoon

AREA OF ORIGIN:Eastern North America

At least twice in the history of North America, goldenseal became wildly popular based on unsubstantiated claims. Hundreds of years ago, after learning of goldenseal's widespread use by Native American healers, colonial herbalists proclaimed it to be a cure for just about everything. In the 1970s, users of illegal drugs believed taking goldenseal would mask the presence of drugs in urine tests. The latter notion has been debunked completely, and scientists have yet to validate goldenseal's value in the illnesses it is supposed to treat, such as colds, infections, and various intestinal disorders.

Unfortunately, wild populations of this delicate woodland plant have been harvested to the point where it has become extremely rare. Although goldenseal is not formally endangered, it is considered threatened in Ontario and has been overharvested in Indiana, West Virginia, and other prime growing areas. Many conservation-minded herbalists suggest substituting Oregon grape root *(Mahonia aquifolium)* for goldenseal, since this plant also contains berberine, and there is absolutely no shortage of either wild or cultivated plants.

Considering goldenseal has not yet been proven to be medically effective, are you, as an individual, willing to participate in the further pilfering of its remaining wild populations? You get to cast your vote when you shop for herbal products, many of which are still made from wild plants. Check product labels carefully to make sure the goldenseal used comes from cultivated plants. Or, consider an alternative, such as echinacea or mahonia root (Oregon grape root).

Medicinal Uses

Despite the absence of scientific data to support its use, many people believe that goldenseal helps with indigestion, colds, and flu, and that it prevents wounds from becoming infected. One of goldenseal's active ingredients, berberine, does have antibiotic properties and may help prevent cancer. However, a second active ingredient, hydrastine, has been linked with side effects, including nausea, miscarriage, and mouth and stomach ulcers. Possibly due to the hydrastine, excessive doses of goldenseal can lead to convulsions and even death.

Even if you follow label directions, you should not take goldenseal for more than a week, and you should not take it at all if you also take prescription drugs to control high blood pressure, if you are pregnant or nursing, or if you have a history of liver problems. Goldenseal is available as capsules, tablets, and liquid extracts, all of which are made from the dried, powdered roots of the plant. Any preparation that contains a high concentration of goldenseal should not be taken for more than three days.

Growing Your Own Goldenseal

Hardy to Zone 5, (see "Know Your Hardiness Zone" on page 85), goldenseal grows wild in Eastern forests, but is very difficult to cultivate without the right ecological niche. If your yard is an open woodland with plenty of shade and rich, moist soil, you might try growing goldenseal from seed or a piece of dormant root. It usually takes about five years for a plant to grow to harvestable size.

HOPS

USES: medicinal, aromatic, ornamental

BOTANICAL NAME: *Humulus lupulus*

OTHER COMMON NAMES: none

AREAS OF ORIGIN: Europe, Asia, North Africa

The classic herb used to flavor beer, hops are the flowering cones of a vigorous vine related to the mulberry. Most of the hops grown today are used in beer-making, as they have been since the ninth century. But as more is learned about this interesting plant, the use of hops as a medicinal herb may be expanding beyond its traditional use as a mild sedative for promoting sound sleep. And, if you're a gardener who is interested in fragrant ornamentals, consider hops, whose vines are also great for covering fences or pergolas. A mighty presence in the garden, hops has the bearing of a grapevine but far fewer problems with pests.

Medicinal Uses

Hops are believed to be a mild sedative, although there is no scientific evidence that validates this fact. However, the aroma of hops, added to a dream pillow, may promote relaxation. And, if the reason you can't sleep is an upset stomach, hops brewed into a weak tea may help.

It has long been known that hops inhibit the spoilage of beer, and extracts from hops are now being used in the manufacture of hot dogs and lunchmeats to deter bacterial growth. Many strains of bacteria are inhibited by the acids in hops, and one recent study has shown that hops pellets (a whole-herb form used in beer-making) killed 90 percent of the *Heliobacter pylori* bacteria in a lab experiment. The liquid extract had no effect. As 75 percent of gastric ulcers are caused by *Heliobacter pylori*, the whole-herb use of hops may be effective in treating this condition. At health food stores, hops are often sold as capsules or tablets. Even when dried, whole hops must be refrigerated or frozen to maintain good medicinal quality.

Aromatic Uses

If you have access to fresh hops, the cone-shaped female flowers may be dried and added to potpourri or dream pillows. Be aware that not everyone likes the fragrance of hops. Abraham Lincoln, however, reportedly was a great fan of hops dream pillows.

Ornamental Uses

Hop vines are very hardy and robust. They can grow 25 feet in a season once they are established in the garden. When tied to poles and allowed to drape over trellises, they provide welcome shade from summer sun. Regular pruning from spring to autumn, while the plants are actively growing, is needed to keep hop vines from taking over a garden. The tiny hairs on the leaves and stems will make you itch, so it's always best to discipline the plants with pruning shears before they grow out of control. In addition to regular green-leafed hops, there is a cultivated variety with chartreuse leaves, 'Aureus,' which is often grown as an ornamental.

Growing Your Own Hops

Hops are hardy to Zone 3 (see "Know Your Hardiness Zone" on page 85), and they grow best where summers are not too hot. At one time, there were large hops-growing industries in New York and Wisconsin, but now, most hops are grown in the Pacific Northwest. To establish a vine, set out a dormant root or rooted cutting in spring, in very fertile, well-worked soil that gets full sun.

Most suppliers sell only female plants, which bear the herb's cone-shaped flowers. If, however, you start hops from seeds, you'll probably get some male plants, which you can eventually eliminate. Regardless of gender, hops usually do not flower until they are three years old. Newly planted hops grow slowly the first year, and take off in the second. In winter, plants die back to the ground.

Each spring, feed vines with an organic or timed-release fertilizer. Gather flowers when they are light brown and have a papery feel, but do not yet have dark spots. Dry them in a slow oven, as is done with culinary herbs (see page 45 for drying techniques). Pack the dried blossoms in an airtight container and store in the freezer.

HOREHOUND

USES:	medicinal, aromatic
BOTANICAL NAME:	*Marrubium vulgare*
OTHER COMMON NAMES:	woolly mint
AREAS OF ORIGIN:	Southern Europe, Western Asia

Hard candies flavored with horehound were long used as cough drops, and you can still buy them at health food stores. Whether or not they actually taste good depends on your personal preferences. Horehound is definitely a bitter herb, and even when made candy-sweet, it has a strong edge to its flavor. The woolly leaves of horehound also make a good addition to dried wreaths or potpourri.

Medicinal Uses

Horehound's ability to soothe coughs is valid. Its active ingredient, marrubiin, increases bronchial secretions, making coughs less persistent and more productive. You can buy horehound cough drops, or use the dried leaves to make a strong tea. Infuse 2 teaspoons of dried horehound leaves in a cup of boiling water, allow it to steep for at least ten minutes, strain, and then mix in enough sugar or honey to make the mixture palatable. Take the tea, a tablespoon at a time, to quiet a cough. Be aware that horehound also has a laxative effect when taken in large doses, so limit your intake to no more than two cups of tea per day.

Aromatic Uses

Horehound has a slight menthol fragrance when used in potpourri. The leaves are woolly with tiny hairs, adding a soft texture to dried wreaths or other types of dried flower arrangements.

Growing Your Own Horehound

A vigorous perennial hardy to Zone 4 (see "Know Your Hardiness Zone" on page 85), horehound is easily grown in any sunny, rather dry site. You can start seeds indoors in late winter and set them out in spring, or begin with a purchased plant. Horehound often does not bloom until its second summer, although you can begin cutting stems for drying from first-season plants. To save horehound for making medicinal teas, look for small clusters of white flowers under the leaves in midsummer, and cut the stems as soon as the flowers begin to open. Dry in the oven or by hanging small bunches in a warm, well-ventilated room. Place the dried leaves, stems, and flowers in an airtight container and store in a dark place. Gather stems to use as dried material before the plants develop mature seeds. Rampant reseeding can be a problem in some areas. In fact, horehound has become a serious weed in Australia, where it has no natural enemies and is shunned by livestock because of its bitter taste. When grown in containers, horehound never gets out of control.

HORSERADISH

USES: medicinal, culinary

BOTANICAL NAME: *Armoracia rusticana*

OTHER COMMON NAMES: redcole, stingnose

AREAS OF ORIGIN: Eastern Europe, Western Asia

Known to the Egyptians but shunned by Europeans for many centuries because of its shocking spiciness, humble horseradish has much to offer. A cinch to grow in any garden, this long-lived plant is grown for its pungent roots. Horseradish is usually used as a spicy condiment, paired with meats or sandwiches, but you can also sniff it to help clear a stuffy nose. And, although horseradish's hot flavor precludes its use in toothpaste, its volatile oils have been found to block the bacterial growth that causes dental plaque.

HORSERADISH'S FAMILY RELATIONS

Often called Japanese horseradish, wasabi (*Wasabia japonica*) is a different plant. It grows more slowly than horseradish, but is also a perennial grown for its pungent roots.

Medicinal Uses

There was a time when holding a piece of horseradish on the forehead was believed to cure a headache—a doubtful remedy, unless the headache was caused by stuffy sinuses, and the person managed to get a good sniff of the freshly cut root. Clearing a stuffy nose is one legitimate medicinal use for this herb. Simply hold some freshly grated or bottled horseradish about four inches from your nose, inhale deeply, and then place a small pinch on your tongue. You should be breathing easier within seconds.

Rich in vitamin C, sulfur, and potassium, horseradish has been taken internally to stimulate digestion. It has antibiotic properties as well, and taking $\frac{1}{2}$ to 1 teaspoon of the grated root three times a day is believed to help clear respiratory and urinary infections. Be aware that ingesting large doses of horseradish could result in sweating or vomiting. It should not be taken internally by those with hypothyroidism.

Culinary Uses

Horseradish is an ideal condiment for giving roast beef added zing. It also enlivens ketchup-based cocktail sauces that accompany seafood and raw vegetables, and when added to mayonnaise, it makes a spicy sandwich spread. Horseradish is never cooked, which destroys its pungency. Raw, grated horseradish can be mixed with vinegar and kept in the refrigerator for up to two months, or you can buy horseradish products, which are sold alongside other condiments in the refrigerated section of most grocery stores.

PURIFYING ROOTS
Peroxidase, an enzyme in horseradish root, is effective in neutralizing common water pollutants. Growing horseradish in soil that is contaminated with phenols, poisonous acidic compounds, can purify the polluted soil.

Whole horseradish roots are sometimes found in stores, and any gardener who grows horseradish has plenty of gratable roots. Store the whole roots in the refrigerator. When the root has been cut and the inner flesh is exposed to the air, a chemical reaction occurs, creating the herb's characteristic pungent fumes. Adding vinegar stops this process. So, if you want the spiciest possible horseradish, grate fresh root into a dish and wait a few minutes before adding vinegar. Glass tableware is recommended, as horseradish reacts with silver.

Growing Your Own Horseradish

A tough perennial hardy to Zone 3 (see "Know Your Hardiness Zone" on page 85), horseradish persists in the garden for many years. Most horseradish has green, strap-shaped leaves. There is a variegated type that has leaves splashed with white, which is worth seeking out. Set out dormant roots in early spring, spacing them at least 12 inches apart. Deep, fertile soil in full sun is best, but horseradish usually manages to make itself at home in less than ideal garden situations. The plants die back in late autumn, which is the best time to dig up the roots. Small pieces of root left behind in the soil will sprout the following spring and grow into new plants, but it's still a good idea to leave at least one parent plant behind to dig up, divide, and replant the following spring. Also, don't worry if you decide not to dig up your horseradish one year. It will keep coming back with no help from you. However, the roots do become woody with age.

HYSSOP
USES: medicinal, ornamental
BOTANICAL NAME: *Hyssopus officinalis*
OTHER COMMON NAMES: none
AREA OF ORIGIN: Southern and Eastern Europe

Hyssop is a sun-loving member of the mint family. It is named four times in the Bible, but historians have concluded that the Biblical hyssop is actually a species of oregano. Yet the herb known as hyssop is an ancient one. Because of its strong medicinal odor, bundles of hyssop branches have long been used to sweep out sickrooms. Hyssop does contain some antiviral compounds, but its practical medicinal uses are limited to using hyssop tea as a gargle to soothe a sore throat. And, although hyssop also has been used as a culinary herb, it does not taste good and few people are inclined to eat it. Today, hyssop's main claim to fame is its physical beauty in the garden, particularly when the plants are in full bloom. Its tiny tubular blue flowers are visited constantly by bees, butterflies, and even hummingbirds.

Medicinal Uses

Hyssop has a bitter taste. Although it contains marrubiin, the same active ingredient present in horehound, it is a less potent source and, therefore, less likely than horehound to calm a cough. However, if you have a sore throat, try gargling with hyssop tea. Add 1 teaspoon of dried hyssop flowers and young leaves to a cup of boiling water. Allow it to steep until lukewarm before straining. Spearmint or peppermint added to this gargle improves its aroma and taste.

Ornamental Uses

Hyssop is often included in herb gardens because it looks so pretty when its blue flowers bloom in early summer. There are also varieties that bloom pink. Plants can grow to 3 feet tall, and the upright blossom-studded stems attract bees and butterflies in droves. Many gardeners believe that hyssop attracts beneficial insects, while repelling those that are harmful to other plants.

Growing Your Own Hyssop

Hyssop is hardy to Zone 4 (see "Know Your Hardiness Zone" on page 85). A perennial that often endures in the garden for many years, hyssop can be grown from seed or from purchased plants. Situate new plants in the garden in spring, in soil that is well drained and not extremely acidic (see "Checking the Soil's pH" on page 88). Hyssop grows into a showy upright mound, although this is one herb that looks best when at least three plants are grown together to form a large mass or hedge. To gather hyssop for medicinal use, clip off the stem tips holding newly opened flowers, and dry them in a warm oven as is done with culinary herbs (see page 45 for drying techniques). Place the dried blossoms in a glass jar or other airtight container, and store in a cool, dark place. Every few years, dig up hyssop in early spring, cut away the old, woody crown and discard it. Promptly replant the healthy young stems found emerging from the base of the plant with a few roots attached.

LAVENDER

USES: medicinal, culinary, aromatic, ornamental

BOTANICAL NAME: *Lavandula angustifolia*

OTHER COMMON NAMES: English lavender

AREA OF ORIGIN: Southern Europe

Lavender smells so good that it's no wonder people are always seeking ways to incorporate it into their lives. A joy in the garden, lavender is the most beloved of aromatic herbs, and few herb enthusiasts consider a season complete without at least one lavender plant to keep the other herbs company. This plant's name, derived from the Latin word *lavare*, meaning "to wash," is perfect for herbal baths. Symbolically, a sprig of lavender has a number of meanings, including dedication, love, and overall virtue. Because the asp, a small venomous snake, was once believed to be attracted to lavender, this herb was at one time associated with feelings of dangerous mistrust as well.

PATRIOTIC PARTNERS
Riveting blue lavender is striking when paired with deep red petunias. Add a touch of white sweet alyssum for an incomparable patriotic combination.

Medicinal Uses

Lavender has only modest medicinal uses, mostly through aromatherapy to aid in relaxation, improve one's tolerance of pain, or simply help lift a blue mood. Its essential oil can be added to massage oil, or you can savor its aroma from a diffuser, tissue, or cotton ball. This is one essential oil that is safe to use on skin with very modest dilution. Lavender essential oil has a mild antibiotic effect, and can be applied directly to small abrasions and insect bites. For sunburn, add a few drops to a teaspoon of aloe gel. When working outdoors, a few lavender stems, crushed and rubbed on your skin, may repel mosquitoes, flies, and other pesky insects.

Culinary Uses

Use lavender flowers sparingly as a garnish for cold desserts, especially ice cream, puddings, and custards. You also can add them to fruit salads in small amounts. Lavender's flavor is quite perfume-like and floral, which tends to compete with the tastes of most foods.

Aromatic Uses

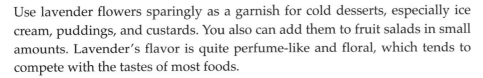

Lavender blossoms are the richest source of its fragrance, but the leaves of many varieties are aromatic, as well. Dry both blossoms and stems for use in potpourri, sachets, and tussie-mussies. You also can dry lavender stems to make smudge sticks. Lavender flowers are at their fragrant peak just as they begin to open. Add lavender essential oil to massage oil, bathwater, or potpourris. The oil can also be used for perfuming a room with this herb's relaxing scent. Lavender essential oil is very stable and usually retains its potency for years.

Ornamental Uses

Typically, lavender plants grow to be 2 feet tall and equally wide. Their gray-green foliage is topped by straight spikes of flowers that bloom in midsummer and range in color from light lavender to deep purple. The plants grow into circular clumps outdoors, or you can grow them in broad containers. Lavender is ideal for growing near a walkway where you can easily pinch a stem tip or flower.

Growing Your Own Lavender

The most fragrant form of lavender, often called English lavender (*L. angustifolia*), has only modest tolerance for extreme cold, and is equally stressed by

LAVENDER'S FAMILY RELATIONS
English lavender has been crossed with other species to create hardy varieties that are tolerant of disease. Sometimes called lavandin, crosses between English lavender (*L. angustifolia*) and spike lavender (*L. latifolia*) have a high content of essential oil. In warm climates, Spanish lavender (*L. stoechas*) is often easier to grow, but its fragrance is weak.

humidity. Although generally hardy in Zones 5 to 8 (see "Know Your Hardiness Zone" on page 85), you may need to grow it in a container so you can move the plants to a cool, protected place such as unheated garage when temperatures drop below 20°F. Lavender craves sun and fresh air, yet grows best in fertile soil with a near neutral pH. (See "Checking the Soil's pH" on page 88.) If your soil is naturally acidic, add lime to pots or beds before planting lavender.

Lavender is difficult to grow from seed; start with plants or rooted cuttings instead. Provide good-quality soil with sand added to improve drainage. Lavender is excellent to grow in containers. Bloom time is usually early to mid summer, which can be prolonged a bit by frequently clipping (and drying) the flowers. One special cultural technique—mulching around plants with 1 inch of sand or coarse pebbles—is especially pleasing to lavender. Instead of cutting garden-grown plants back in autumn, wait until early spring to trim old plants to improve their shape. That way, the old stems will help shelter the base of the plant from harsh winter weather. To increase your supply of plants, take stem cuttings in summer, strip off the lowest leaves, and set the groomed cuttings in damp, sandy potting soil to root. Plants usually do not bloom well until their second year in the garden. Specimens more than five years old often lose their vigor and are best replaced.

LEMON BALM

USES: medicinal, culinary, aromatic

BOTANICAL NAME: *Melissa officinalis*

OTHER COMMON NAMES: Melissa

AREAS OF ORIGIN: Southern Europe, North Africa

A robust perennial herb with a knack for making itself at home almost anywhere, lemon balm has an important modern medicinal use fighting certain viruses, as well as a more ancient one for calming nerves. This herb's use goes back more than twelve centuries, and it has an excellent safety record for both internal and external use. The lemon-scented leaves also have long been used to attract bees to new hives, perhaps because they contain a compound similar to one found in the glands of worker honeybees.

Medicinal Uses

Water-soluble compounds within lemon balm leaves have been found to be effective in treating both oral herpes, which causes painful mouth sores and fever blisters, and genital herpes, which causes similar lesions in the genital area. Commercial creams made with lemon balm are sold at health food stores but may be difficult to find. At home, you can make an alcohol-based extract (see "Making Liquid Extracts" on page 32) and apply it to affected areas four times daily at the first sign of trouble. Or, if it is summer and you have plenty of fresh lemon balm but don't want to wait two weeks to make an extract, you can prepare a strong lemon balm tea and use it the same way.

Lemon balm tea, extract, and capsules all are effective at reducing anxiety and helping you to calm down in times of stress. Herbalists often use lemon balm to help with stress-induced hypertension, especially if the person is experiencing panic attacks. In this situation, taking lemon balm as a tea, extract, or capsule three times daily for two to four weeks is the typical intervention. You can also try lemon balm tea for treating a simple headache.

Culinary Uses

Few people truly enjoy the taste of lemon balm, but you can chop up small amounts to add color and flavor to cheese spreads, or marinate a few sprigs in otherwise uninteresting white wine to impart a more complex flavor.

Aromatic Uses

You can enjoy the citrusy aroma of lemon balm indoors by using the fresh stems in flower arrangements. Dried leaves may be added to potpourri, although another lemon-scented herb, lemon verbena, is far superior for this purpose. In the garden, make a habit of stopping by your lemon balm and crushing a few leaves in your hands for simple smelling pleasure.

Growing Your Own Lemon Balm

Any friend who has lemon balm will gladly give you a rooted cutting, or you can start with a purchased plant. Lemon balm is hardy to Zones 4 to 9 (see "Know Your Hardiness Zone" on page 85). It grows up to 36 inches tall in either sun or partial shade. In fact, it grows so well that it is often considered weedy; however, unwanted plants are easy to pull out. Lemon balm emerges from winter dormancy in spring. The best time to gather leaves is early summer, just before the plants flower.

To dry lemon balm for use in tea, gather long stems, strip off the lowest leaves, and hang them to dry in small bunches. Remove the leaves when the stems are nearly crisp, and store them in an airtight container. Making lemon balm extract is recommended in the early summer, when its fresh leaves are in peak condition.

LEMON VERBENA
USES: culinary, aromatic
BOTANICAL NAME: *Aloysia triphylla*
OTHER COMMON NAMES: yerba Louisa
AREAS OF ORIGIN: Argentina, Chile, Peru

Lemon verbena is a tropical shrub that quickly becomes a beloved member of any collection of herbs. Popular in teas and potpourri, or for the simple pleasure of picking a leaf and crushing it between your fingers, this herb is almost more "lemony" than lemons, meaning it has a stronger citrusy smell than lemons do. In most climates, lemon verbena must be grown in containers because it cannot tolerate cold, but it is well worth this small amount of trouble. The narrow green leaves are the usable plant part. When grown in warm climates, lemon verbena often produces tiny white flowers in late summer; however, in most areas, the plants seldom, if ever, bloom. When the plants do bloom, the tiny white flowers look nothing at all like the common annual and perennial flowers that gardeners call verbenas.

Culinary Uses

Lemon verbena's strong lemony scent makes it a refreshing addition to tea, hot or iced, and you can use it to mask the less desirable flavors of some herbal teas used for medicinal purposes. For a festive touch, freeze individual leaves in ice cubes and add them to cold drinks. Finely chopped leaves will add a lemony accent to cakes, muffins, salad dressings, and marinades. In Asian recipes that call for lemon grass, lemon verbena leaves are an acceptable substitute. Lemon verbena's flavor is always best fresh or very lightly cooked.

Aromatic Uses

Fresh or dried, no other green herb can match lemon verbena for its clean citrus scent. Gather stems or individual leaves to dry and add to potpourri and sachets. Include fresh leaves in tussie-mussies, and then allow the entire arrangement to dry. In times past, women would tuck stems of lemon verbena into their hats, sleeves, or dress bodices to make the most of its alluring fragrance, which was believed to promote intimacy.

Growing Your Own Lemon Verbena

Although lemon verbena is a long-lived perennial, it cannot tolerate having its roots frozen. So, in all but Zones 8 to 10 (see "Know Your Hardiness Zone" on page 85), it should be grown in containers that can be brought indoors for the winter. Begin with a purchased plant. When grown outdoors in hot climates, plants can reach 6 feet or more, but in containers, 3 feet or so is an average height. The plants prefer plenty of sun, rich yet well-drained soil, and regular feeding during summer months.

It's wise to cut back plants by about half their size once or twice during summer, both to gather the leaves and stems and to promote new growth. In winter, plants shed their leaves and become dormant. Keep the soil only very lightly moist during this period, and increase water when new growth appears in spring. To propagate lemon verbena, root new stem cuttings taken in early summer.

LOVAGE

USES: medicinal, culinary

BOTANICAL NAME: *Levisticum officinale*

OTHER COMMON NAMES: none

AREA OF ORIGIN: Southern Europe

Commonly known as the celery herb, lovage tastes and smells like celery, but it is much easier to grow in a garden. Every part of the plant is edible, including its stems, leaves, seeds, and even roots, which have diuretic properties and are one of the oldest known remedies for kidney stones. Best of all, a single stately lovage plant will persist in the garden for years, requiring little attention while at the same time offering a long season of tasty tidbits for soups, stews, salads, and sandwiches.

Medicinal Uses

Like many herbs, lovage was once thought of as a cure-all, appropriate for every ailment. But by modern standards, the only practical medicinal use for this herb is to increase urination for the purpose of flushing out the kidneys and bladder. The most potent plant part is the root, which can be dried and used to brew a diuretic infusion, using 2 teaspoons of dried root per cup of water. Or you can steep 2 teaspoons of dried lovage leaves in a cup of water to make a diuretic tea. Because the point of using lovage or any other diuretic is to flush out the body's urinary system, be sure to drink additional water as part of the therapy.

Culinary Uses

Any dish that calls for celery can accommodate lovage instead. However, because of lovage's strong flavor, use only half as much as you would celery. Lovage is excellent in potato salad, sprinkled over buttered new potatoes, chopped into sandwich spreads, or added to soups and stews. Like celery, lovage goes well with poultry or fish. The young leaves offer the best flavor, which is a cross between celery and parsley. You can also harvest the young stems, blanch them for a minute in boiling water, and eat them like asparagus. Lovage seeds are edible, too, and can be used in place of celery seeds in any recipe.

Lovage plants are quite large, and a single plant will produce plenty of leaves for fresh cooking and for freezing or drying. Many cooks chop the leaves and freeze them in ice cubes (see page 45), but they also can be dried. Just be sure to store the dried leaves in a dark place, because exposure to light will turn them from green to yellow. Lovage seeds retain their flavor for two years or more when stored in a cool, dark place.

Growing Your Own Lovage

A long-lived perennial hardy to Zone 3 (see "Know Your Hardiness Zone" on page 85), lovage asks only for rich soil that retains moisture well and some shade from hot afternoon sun when grown in hot climates. Lovage is more shade tolerant than other herbs, and also much larger, often reaching 6 feet tall when in full flower. For these reasons, it is an ideal plant for the rear of the herb garden. You can start lovage from seed, or begin with dormant roots or one-year-old plants set out in early spring. Provide young plants with plenty of water, and allow them to grow freely their first year, pinching off leaves only occasionally to use in the kitchen. In their second and subsequent years, plants will be much larger, producing spikes of yellow flowers in midsummer. These flowers can be allowed to mature if you want lovage seeds. However, if you prefer a second flush of tender new leaves instead, cut the plants back close to the ground when the blossom spikes appear. Just in time for autumn, a new crop of stems and leaves will be perfect for picking.

Healthy lovage plants often persist in the garden for many years, returning early in the spring after becoming completely dormant in winter. If you want to rejuvenate an old plant or increase your supply of lovage, dig up the plant in early spring, break off 6-inch-long sections of root, and replant them about 2 feet apart.

GOLDFINCH GOLDMINE
One of the best reasons to allow lovage to produce seeds is to attract colorful goldfinches, which munch on the seeds during the second half of summer.

MARJORAM

USES: medicinal, culinary, aromatic, ornamental

BOTANICAL NAME: *Origanum majorana*

OTHER COMMON NAMES: sweet marjoram, knotted marjoram

AREAS OF ORIGIN: North Africa, Western Asia

The daintiest of the oregano tribe, marjoram has a flavor often described as clean, sweet, and savory. To the ancient Greeks, marjoram was the herb of marital bliss. Brides and grooms often wore marjoram garlands on their heads. This herb is sometimes called knotted marjoram because the flower buds are round balls, or knots, awkwardly studded with tiny white flowers. You can use this characteristic to confirm that you do, indeed, have sweet marjoram rather than a related oregano, because marjoram is the only oregano cousin with this flower type.

Medicinal Uses

Marjoram is not a major player among medicinal herbs, but a tea brewed from its leaves may help alleviate indigestion and headaches. Drinking the tea may also increase tolerance for or speed recovery from stress.

Culinary Uses

Marjoram is one herb that deserves wider use in cooking. Happily, dried marjoram delivers flavor that is nearly equal to the fresh version. Think of marjoram as tamed oregano, and use it with confidence in pasta and pizza, or as an accent for potatoes or potato soup. Marjoram works well with eggs or cheese dishes, too, and a light sprinkling adds savory flavor to cream sauces or cream soups. Most vegetables pair well with marjoram, and the little flowers make interesting garnishes for any course. Marjoram also makes a delicious herb butter, and the flowering tops are a pretty addition to herbal vinegar. When drying marjoram for kitchen use, use the slow oven method (see page 46) to retain good color and most of this herb's essential oils. Marjoram's flavor is usually best just as its flower buds form.

Aromatic Uses

Use stems of marjoram in potpourris, sachets, tussie-mussies, and herbal wreaths. When added to sweet pillows, marjoram was once believed to encourage dreams of your heart's true love. You can dry short marjoram stems on screens or hang small bunches of longer stems in a warm place until dry. (See page 45 for drying techniques.)

Ornamental Uses

A compact plant that never grows more than 16 inches tall, marjoram can be groomed into a pretty groundcover provided it is well pleased with its soil and site. Full sun and a gritty, fast-draining soil are best. Marjoram also grows well in containers, where it is good to grow with other culinary herbs.

Growing Your Own Marjoram

Hardy to Zone 9 (see "Know Your Hardiness Zone" on page 85), marjoram can't tolerate subfreezing temperatures, so it is usually grown as an annual. You can start with seed sown indoors in late winter, but germination is usually only about 50 percent, and early growth is very slow. A faster option is to buy new plants in spring.

Set marjoram plants out just after the last spring frost. Feed them monthly with an all-purpose plant food, or more often if plants are grown in containers. Plants that wilt for more than a few hours in midday need more water. Cut the stems often, which encourages the plants to grow new branches. Or you can wait until just before flower buds form and harvest stems by shearing back the plants by two-thirds their size. Sufficient stems for a second cutting should develop by early autumn. Marjoram often develops root rot when kept indoors through winter, but if you have a very sunny window, keeping it inside is certainly worth a try.

MEADOWSWEET

USES: medicinal, aromatic, ornamental

BOTANICAL NAME: *Filipendula ulmaria*

OTHER COMMON NAMES: queen of the meadow, bridewort

AREA OF ORIGIN: Europe

From its beginning as a wild plant of Europe's moist meadows, meadowsweet became a leading flavoring herb for beer in the Middle Ages. The almond-scented flowers were also strewn over floors, and meadowsweet teas were popular remedies for a long list of intestinal ailments. In 1839, salicylic acid (an ingredient in aspirin) was synthesized from meadowsweet flowers; however, by modern standards, the amount of salicylic acid contained in meadowsweet flowers is far below therapeutic doses. These days, meadowsweet is grown primarily as an ornamental, appreciated for its tall flower clusters and the historical heritage it brings to the garden.

Medicinal Uses

Teas brewed from meadowsweet buds and flowers—2 tablespoons of dried herb per cup of boiling water—are still used to treat fevers, as well as to reduce problems with heartburn. This is a situation in which the whole herb is likely more useful than its derivatives. If you cannot tolerate aspirin, you should probably bypass meadowsweet, too.

Aromatic Uses

Used in fresh flower arrangements, the sweet almond scent of meadowsweet is strong enough to perfume a room. Dried and crushed, the flowers make good filler material for potpourri, although the scent often fades after the blossoms are dry.

Ornamental Uses

Plants sold by species name (*F. ulmaria*) grow into large clumps, and may reach 7 feet tall when in full bloom. They prefer partial shade or filtered sun, and rich, moist soil. Improved cultivated varieties that are popular among gardeners include 'Flore Pleno' meadowsweet, which grows only 3 feet tall and produces very large white flower clusters. In addition, two cultivated varieties are grown primarily for their showy leaves. 'Aurea' meadowsweet has chartreuse-green foliage, while the leaves of 'Variegata' feature golden stripes and splashes.

Growing Your Own Meadowsweet

Easily grown in Zones 3 to 8 (see "Know Your Hardiness Zone" on page 85), meadowsweet needs plenty of moisture, so it is a good plant for low areas that tend to stay damp. Before setting out purchased plants in spring, add a little lime to the soil to raise its pH to near alkaline levels of around 7.0. (See "Checking the Soil's pH" on page 88.) Established clumps thrive with little care, and the flowers attract small beneficial insects. Meadowsweet becomes dormant in winter, and the plants emerge anew in mid spring.

MINT

USES:	medicinal, culinary, aromatic
BOTANICAL NAME:	*Mentha* species
OTHER COMMON NAMES:	none
AREAS OF ORIGIN:	Europe, Asia

You can use the bracing aroma of mint to refresh your tea, your hair, your kitchen countertops, or even a stale closet. There are many types of mint, including some that carry the subtle scents of apple, pineapple, or chocolate, but the two mints that most herbalists cannot do without are peppermint (*Mentha x piperita*) and spearmint (*M. spicata*). Of all the mints, peppermint has the strongest minty aroma, so it is the best choice for fragrant bouquets, freshening the air, or for using dried in wreaths or sachets. Spearmint is the most often-used culinary mint, as well as a vigorous grower. These and other mints also deter flies and other unwanted insects, and they are herbal medicine's first remedy for minor problems with digestion.

MINT'S FAMILY RELATIONS

Pineapple mint has little flavor but eye-catching leaves. Japanese mint's peppermint-tasting leaves make great aromatic groundcover. Inedible pennyroyal is a fine insect repellent.

Medicinal Uses

Most mints contain respectable amounts of vitamins A and C, plus they are rich in antioxidants. The menthol in mint aids digestion and can even calm intestinal cramps. Plus, no herbal tea tastes as good as mint tea, which has an impeccable safety record. In addition to drinking mint tea straight, you can add mint to teas made with less flavorful herbs for a better flavor.

Culinary Uses

You can use any type of mint for cooking, although spearmint is usually the

first choice because of its fresh, clean flavor. Young leaves, gathered from stem tips, have the sprightliest flavor. Any cold drink, including chilled milk, can get a gentle lift from a sprig of crushed mint. In salads, mint partners well with fruits such as apples, pears, and strawberries. It is essential in many Middle Eastern dishes, from cucumber-yogurt sauce to tabbouleh, the chilled salad made from cracked wheat, parsley, mint, and tomatoes. A little mint added to cream sauce makes a delectable topping for steamed asparagus, peas, or other vegetables. Do be careful not to partner mint with garlic or onions, which simply makes a poor match.

Aromatic Uses

When stems are gathered in early summer, before plants flower or become stressed by hot weather, mint can be dried very easily by hanging the stems in small bunches in a warm, dark place. You may want to use an oven method to dry mint intended for the kitchen to minimize the possibility of molds or tiny creatures hiding in the leaves. However, mint that is to be used for potpourri or sachets holds its aroma well when air dried and then stored in airtight containers. Use fresh stems of mint liberally in flower arrangements of all sizes. Mint is also a good herb to incorporate into herbal wreaths.

Growing Your Own Mint

Most mints are vigorous growers that spread by sending out wandering stems an inch or two below the soil's surface. For this reason, many gardeners prefer to grow mints in containers, or in small beds where their spread can be easily kept in check. Hardy to Zone 5 (see "Know Your Hardiness Zone" on page 85) and accepting of either full sun or partial shade, mints begin growing first thing in spring, flower in midsummer, and then regrow in autumn if they are pruned back and given a good dose of water and fertilizer. If your winters are too cold for mint, grow it in containers and move the plants to a cool room in late autumn. With only occasional watering during the winter months, the pots will be ready to move back outdoors first thing in spring. Peppermint is a hybrid, so it does not produce true seeds and must be propagated from rooted cuttings. Spearmint is a good seed producer, but the best strains also are propagated from rooted cuttings. In both cases, it is best to begin with plants grown by a nursery that is run by someone with a good nose for mints.

MONARDA

USES: medicinal, culinary, aromatic, ornamental

BOTANICAL NAME: *Monarda citriodora, M. didyma*

OTHER COMMON NAMES: bee balm, bergamot, horsebalm, Oswego tea

AREA OF ORIGIN: Eastern North America

Try as we might to be clear on plant names, when it comes to various species of monarda, there is no way to win. This jolly band of native North American plants, long enjoyed as tea by the continent's ancestral tribes, includes some plants that make a citrusy tea, others with a mintier flavor paired with wildly beautiful flowers, and still others that taste strongly of thyme. So, if you want a certain monarda for a specific purpose, you may have to let yourself be led by your nose through various offerings at local nurseries. Strains with strong citrus flavors are often called bergamot because their aromas are similar to those of the tropical tree orange bergamot (*Citrus aurantium*).

Medicinal Uses

Like many of the healing arts used by Native American tribes, the historical medicinal uses for monarda have largely been forgotten. Tea made from the leaves was used as a cure-all for disorders ranging from stomachaches to heart trouble.

Culinary Uses

Monarda leaves make a great tea herb, and they combine well with other mints, chamomile, and rose hips. In fact, monarda tea, which was in great demand following the Boston Tea Party, is sometimes called Oswego tea because a Shaker community based near Oswego, New York, became its major supplier. To dry the leaves for tea, gather stems in early summer and rinse them well to clean them. When dry, pick off individual leaves and dry them in the oven (see page 46). Monarda's shaggy flowers are edible, too, and the bright petals make colorful additions to summer salads, particularly fruit and gelatin salads.

Aromatic Uses

Both leaves and dried blossoms of monarda can be added to potpourri. You can dry the colorful petals or the whole flowers, which look quite dramatic.

Ornamental Uses

Monarda's common name of bee balm is well earned, because its flowers strongly attract honeybees as well as hummingbirds. It's best to locate plants away from entryways to allow space for flying visitors. And unlike most herbs, which crave sun, monarda prefers partial shade. Bloom time is usually midsummer, and plants typically bloom only once each year. Monarda makes an excellent bed partner with another beautiful native North American flower, garden phlox (*Phlox paniculata*).

Growing Your Own Monarda

Many monarda strains can be grown from seed, but the best forms of the biggest and brightest blooming species, *M. didyma,* are propagated from stem cuttings. The main reason to seek out an improved variety for your garden is that monardas in general are susceptible to a common disease called powdery mildew, which causes numerous white patches to form on the leaves. Look for varieties known to be resistant to this disease if it is prevalent in your area. All strains are hardy to Zone 4 (see "Know Your Hardiness Zone" on page 85). Set out plants in spring in a site that tends to stay constantly moist. Plants usually grow to about 3 feet tall.

OREGANO

USES: medicinal, culinary, ornamental

BOTANICAL NAME: *Origanum* species

OTHER COMMON NAMES: wild marjoram

AREAS OF ORIGIN: Europe, Asia

Oregano means "joy of the mountains," and the Greek physician Dioscorides used it as a medicine. An essential herb in Italian, Greek, and Mexican cooking, oregano is actually more than one plant. In fact, the oregano you buy at the supermarket is likely to be a mixture of several types of oregano. Unfortunately, the oreganos with the best flavor have a low tolerance for cold winter weather, while hardier strains grow with amazing vigor, but often lack flavor. Why not have both? The best culinary form, often called Greek oregano and classified as *O. heracleoticum* or *O. vulgare* can be grown much like its close cousin, marjoram. Exuberant and hardy wild oregano, *O. vulgare,* makes a lush clump of green in the garden, and produces plenty of pink flower clusters for herbal wreaths and potpourri.

Medicinal Uses

Oregano is remarkably rich in antioxidants, which help prevent cancer and may be effective in regulating blood pressure and reducing inflammation from arthritis. There is no clear scientific information on taking oregano as a supplement, but high doses of some of its active compounds can be toxic; however, don't be afraid to use oregano liberally in foods. The amount used in cooking falls far below levels that may pose a health risk. Some studies suggest that certain antioxidants in oregano counteract naturally occurring carcinogens (cancer-causing chemicals) that we ingest as a normal part of our diets.

Culinary Uses

Pizza, spaghetti sauce, and Greek salad dressings depend on Greek oregano for their savory flavor. Oregano is also a fine herb to chop into herb butters or cheese spreads, or use to make herbal vinegar. Its dried, flaked leaves make a flavorful addition to dry rubs for meat, fish, and poultry. Oregano also makes a good addition to chili and various salsas, and it's an excellent herb to chop and sprinkle over egg dishes such as omelets or quiches. In summer, a few weeks after the weather turns warm, gather the plant's short stems and dry them in the oven before storing your oregano for winter use. (See page 46 for drying technique.)

Ornamental Uses

Wild oregano produces stiff stems topped by clusters of pink flowers in early summer. Either fresh or dried in bunches, the flowers make good filler for tussie-mussies and potpourri, or for decorating herbal wreaths.

Growing Your Own Oregano

Wild oregano is generally winter hardy to Zone 5, while Greek oregano often succumbs to cold north of Zone 7 (see "Know Your Hardiness Zone" on page 83). Once your find a truly flavorful strain (which may require a little hunting), you probably won't mind going to the trouble of growing Greek oregano in containers that can be brought into a cool garage or other cool protected place during the winter. The best hunting tip is to shop for plants in the spring, and actually taste and sniff a leaf before buying. All oreganos grow best in good sun, and hot weather intensifies their flavors and aromas. However, don't expect a plant with no flavor in the spring to taste radically better in midsummer. If you live in Zones 9 or 10, you can get good oregano flavor from two plants that are totally unrelated to Greek oregano—Mexican oregano (*Lippia graveolens*) or Cuban oregano (*Plectranthus amboinicus*).

OREGANO'S FAMILY RELATIONS
Marjoram (*O. majorana*) is an annual oregano that offers dependable flavor, although it must be started anew each spring.

PARSLEY

USES: medicinal, culinary, ornamental

BOTANICAL NAME: *Petroselinum crispum*

OTHER COMMON NAMES: none

AREA OF ORIGIN: Middle East

More than a pretty decoration for the edge of a plate, parsley is nutritious, flavorful, and carries with it a long history of meanings associated with people's most heartfelt hopes and fears. The ancient Greeks, for example, linked parsley with honorable death and planted it on graves. Many centuries later, parsley became an important healing herb and was used for the treatment of maladies ranging from kidney stones to the plague. Today, we eat more parsley than

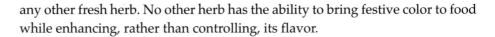

any other fresh herb. No other herb has the ability to bring festive color to food while enhancing, rather than controlling, its flavor.

Medicinal Uses

Teas made from parsley seeds and leaves have long been used as diuretics and antihistamines. But for practical purposes, parsley is best regarded as a nutritional rather than medicinal herb. Very high in vitamin A, vitamin C, and iron, parsley is also a good source of boron and fluorine, which help build strong bones.

Culinary Uses

Few dishes outside the dessert category cannot benefit from at least a light sprinkling of parsley. Parsley's flavor weakens when it is cooked, but its nutritional riches remain. For this reason, use parsley liberally in grain or pasta dishes that can benefit from its flavor and color, and then add a little more just before the dish is served. Parsley can be substituted for basil in pesto, and it is always an excellent partner for either garlic or mint. Curly parsley is pretty and versatile, but many cooks prefer the flavor of flat-leafed parsley, sometimes called Italian parsley.

Unfortunately, parsley loses much of its flavor when dried. To preserve an abundance from your garden or leftovers from the store, freeze the stems in freezer bags or clean, dry airtight containers, loosely packed. The parsley will be wilted when thawed, but it should still have much of its fresh flavor and color.

PARSLEY CATERPILLARS
Colorful green caterpillars with bright yellow markings (future swallowtail butterflies) often feed on parsley. Gently transfer these caterpillars to a spare plant or two—you'll have your parsley and butterflies, too.

Ornamental Uses

Standard parsley varieties grow into 15-inch-tall mounds, which are topped by flower clusters in the spring of their second year. You can also grow dwarf varieties, which are so compact and pretty that they make a lovely edging for any sunny bed. Parsley will grow in containers, too, and looks especially beautiful when combined with other herbs such as basil and thyme.

Growing Your Own Parsley

Parsley is classified as a biennial, which means that it usually does not flower and produce seeds until its second year, after which it typically dies. Yet most gardeners grow parsley as an annual by starting seeds very early in the spring. Seeds sprout best if they are soaked in water for a couple of days first, a procedure that removes chemicals found in the seed coats that inhibit germination. Most garden centers also sell parsley seedlings, and it's best to buy them early and set them out right away. When parsley must be transplanted, do so when the plants are young, and disturb the roots as little as possible. You can begin picking individual stems within a few weeks, and new stems will continue to appear well into autumn. Healthy parsley plants often survive winter in a dormant state, as far north as Zone 5 (see "Know Your Hardiness Zone" on page 85). One-year-old plants produce lovely dome-shaped clusters of greenish-yellow flowers in late spring, which make good additions to fresh or dried flower arrangements.

PARSLEY'S FAMILY RELATIONS
In addition to curly and Italian parsley, there is Hamburg parsley. It has edible leaves and a root that can be eaten like a parsnip. Chinese/ Mexican parsley is another relation (see "Cilantro/Coriander" on page 137).

PENNYROYAL

USES: aromatic

BOTANICAL NAME: *Mentha pulegium, Hedeoma pulegioides*

OTHER COMMON NAMES: coyote mint

AREAS OF ORIGIN: Europe, Eastern United States

Two different plants go by the name of pennyroyal—English pennyroyal (*Mentha pulegium*) and American pennyroyal (*Hedeoma pulegioides*). Both herbs are related to mints and have long been used by herbalists on both continents to treat stomach problems, promote sweating to help break fevers, and to end unwanted pregnancies. In addition, pennyroyal is used as an insect repellent; in fact, its botanical name, *pulegium,* is derived from the Latin word for flea. But in truth, most of the traditional uses for pennyroyal are extremely dangerous. Reports of death and illness due to pennyroyal ingestion were first published in 1897 and continue to this day. Young women, perhaps having read of pennyroyal's use in promoting spontaneous abortion, have ended up requiring kidney transplants after drinking the tea or ingesting the essential oil. Babies given pennyroyal tea to treat colic have died.

So what good is pennyroyal? The fresh stems, braided into a flea collar for your dog or cat, or rubbed on your clothes as you brave gnats and mosquitoes, make a nice-smelling insect repellent. This is a far different approach from taking pennyroyal internally, which should never be considered, or using the essential oil, which is so strong that it has no practical uses. Even in natural flea control collars, it should be used in carefully controlled amounts.

Aromatic Uses

Use the fresh stems of this mint cousin to repel insects from outdoor environments. Grab a handful and crush them to release their aroma, or braid them into the band of your garden hat. Pennyroyal contains monoterpene pulegone, which repels insects. Sprigs of pennyroyal braided into a pet collar are safe, but do not get carried away and overdo it with this herb. Too much pennyroyal, for either pets or people, can have dangerous side effects, including convulsions, liver damage, or even death. However, these dangers are not associated with the occasional use of fresh pennyroyal stems as an aromatic. It's fine to breathe this herb's fresh fragrance, but do not take any form of pennyroyal internally or rub the essential oil directly onto your skin or on the skin of pets. After handling fresh pennyroyal, promptly wash your hands.

Growing Your Own Pennyroyal

American pennyroyal is an annual herb that often reseeds itself, while European pennyroyal is perennial, hardy to Zone 5 (see "Know Your Hardiness Zone" on page 85). If you grow either one of these plants, make sure they are labeled so they are not confused with other herbs. Or grow them in containers that are kept in a sunny spot. The aroma of pennyroyal is very minty and refreshing, so crushing a few leaves or stems deters insects while perfuming the outdoor air.

ROSE

USES: culinary, aromatic, ornamental

BOTANICAL NAME: *Rosa* species

OTHER COMMON NAMES: French rose, rose hips

AREAS OF ORIGIN: every continent, but especially the Middle East

Beloved for their elegant good looks and inspiring fragrance, roses have been associated with love since before the time of Cleopatra, who deeply believed in their romantic powers. There are hundreds of rose species, native to nearly every part of the world, but only a few are of special interest to herbalists. Roses that produce big crops of tart-tasting fruits, known as rose hips, are a favorite of tea drinkers, while those with the strongest fragrance are sought after for potpourri. Yet rose petals of any type can be gathered and dried for this purpose, including roses that come from florists. However, when rose parts are to be used in foods or teas, it is important that the plants be grown without pesticides. Florists' roses, while beautiful, are often heavily treated with chemicals.

Culinary Uses

Rose hips, which are rich in vitamin C, B, E, and K, have a tart, zingy flavor, so they are usually used in sweetened teas, syrups, jellies, and various desserts. To dry rose hips that you grow and gather yourself, cut them open with a sharp knife and remove the seeds before drying in a warm oven. Rose petals are edible, too, although you may want to snip off the bottom quarter inch of each petal, which often tastes bitter. Because of their strong floral flavor, rose petals are usually used as garnishes for salads, sandwiches, and desserts.

Aromatic Uses

It takes thousands of rose blossoms to produce an ounce of essential oil, so buying some is a good investment if you love the aroma of roses. Meanwhile, be sure to dry the petals from roses and save them for use in potpourris and sachets. Pull the flowers apart and dry the petals individually, laying them out on a flat surface. Even petals picked up off the ground are worth drying. Quick drying in a dry heated place helps preserve the color of the petals. Dark-colored petals are less likely to show scratches and bruises than petals from white or pink roses.

Ornamental Uses

With thousands of roses to choose from, any gardener with an available spot of sun where the soil is fertile and nicely drained can grow at least one type of rose. Roses vary in size and form, ranging from small miniature roses that can be grown in containers to huge ramblers that develop canes (stiff stems) more than 20 feet long. Their fragrance varies, too (some roses have no fragrance at all). To make matters more complicated, many roses bloom only once each season, usually in early summer, while others bloom off and on from early summer until autumn. How you showcase a rose encompasses all of these factors, as well as its color.

In an herb garden, you might use a large climbing rose, trained to grow on a fence or trellis, or you can anchor a bed of herbs with a single rose that grows into a rounded bush. Lavender is often used as a companion plant for roses. You can also give roses their own bed and hem the edges with creeping thyme. There are many more possibilities since roses thrive in the same kind of sunny sites that are pleasing to most herbs.

Growing Your Own Roses

The world of roses is divided into numerous types, including miniatures, climbers, ramblers, rugosas, old roses (which have been in cultivation for decades or even centuries), floribundas, and the most popular roses of all called hybrid teas. Hybrid teas, developed 100 years ago by crossing three species, have the classic shape of florists' roses. There are hundreds of named varieties.

There are many more types of roses, but the three that are most often used as herbs are rugosa roses (*Rosa rugosa*), which bear large, well-flavored "hips," or berries; the seductively scented damask rose (*R. damascena*); and the very old apothecary rose (*R. gallica*), which has been famed for its perfume for thousands of years.

Native to Asia, rugosa roses are vigorous upright bushes that are hardy to Zone 3. (See "Know Your Hardiness Zone" on page 85.) They are easy to grow in a garden because they are naturally resistant to common rose diseases. Rugosas bear small, simple flowers in shades of red and pink. Some of the newer hybrid rugosas are fragrant, featuring a spicy clove scent.

Damask roses are the roses of ancient Persia, and they are usually hardy to

KEEPING SECRETS
In addition to being
the flower of love,
the rose is symbolic of
secrets. A rose hung
over a table is a sign
that the conversation
is meant to be
confidential. Should
you be told that
certain information
is *sub rosa*, which
translates as "under
the rose," you are
being let in on
a secret.

Zone 4. Their fragrance is rich and enticing, but most roses of this species bloom only once a year in early summer, and primarily in shades of pink. The 'Celsiana' variety also produces brightly colored hips that can be used like those from rugosa roses. Most damask roses grow into large bushes.

Gallica roses were used medicinally in ancient Rome. Most gallicas produce fragrant pink or red flowers followed by colorful hips. Their cold hardiness varies, with some being hardy to Zone 4, and others to Zone 6. Many gallicas grow into lanky bushes, or you can train them to climb on a trellis.

To grow any of these roses, begin in early spring by setting out dormant plants that are just beginning to grow new leaf buds. Amend the planting hole with plenty of good compost or other organic matter, spread the roots carefully, and water well to make sure no air pockets are left around the planted roots. Fertilize newly planted and established roses in early summer, soon after the plants show vigorous new growth.

With these and other roses that bloom once a year, it is best to prune them in midsummer after the flowers fade to remove old canes and shape the plants. However, they do not require the rigorous pruning needed by hybrid teas and other reblooming roses. Do keep the plants supplied with water during hot, dry periods in the summer. If you plan to use your rose hips in teas, collect them in late summer or autumn, after they turn orange or red, but before they become shriveled or brown.

ROSEMARY

USES: medicinal, culinary, aromatic, ornamental

BOTANICAL NAME: *Rosmarinus officinalis*

OTHER COMMON NAMES: none

AREA OF ORIGIN: Western Europe

Rosemary has long been known as the herb of remembrance. Simply inhaling rosemary's piney aroma stimulates brain chemistry, which can make thinking a shade clearer or more efficient. This ability has stood up well under scientific scrutiny. Rosemary is also a classic culinary herb, and it contains so many antioxidants that it makes a serviceable meat preservative. Beautiful as a garnish or standing in the garden, rosemary leaves are popular additions to bath packets and sweet pillows, or they can be woven into herbal wreaths. It is also the definitive herb to tuck into a letter to a loved one who is far away to signify remembrance.

THE SEASIDE HERB
Rosemary is one of the few herbs that tolerates salt spray, so it can be grown near the beach. In fact, its genus name, *Rosmarinus*, is derived from two Latin words meaning "dew of the sea."

Medicinal Uses

The antioxidants in rosemary may help relieve arthritic inflammation and prevent the formation of tumors. The best way to ingest rosemary is in foods or as a minor addition to herbal teas. Large amounts of rosemary (more than one tablespoon of chopped fresh leaves) taken at once can irritate the stomach and may cause kidney problems.

Culinary Uses

Rosemary has such assertive flavor that it dominates dishes in which it is used. Often paired with pork or poultry, rosemary is also a wonderful topping for the flat Italian bread known as focaccia, as well as a fine complement for roasted potatoes. Try adding a pinch or two to beans to bring out their savory flavor. Rosemary is one of the easiest culinary herbs to dry, either by hanging its long branches in small bunches or by drying small springs on screens or another flat surface. (See drying techniques on page 45.) Stored in airtight containers, dried rosemary will keep its flavor for many months.

Aromatic Uses

To treat depression, massage therapists sometimes add 3 drops of rosemary essential oil to 1 tablespoon of unscented massage oil. For a refreshing bath, add dried or fresh rosemary leaves to a bath packet. Mix dried rosemary in potpourris, or make a strong tea to use as a hair rinse. Personally, I utilize the brain-enhancing properties of rosemary by pinching a sprig into tiny pieces and keeping them in a little bowl on my desk when I'm tackling a difficult task. Even if it does not make me smarter, it certainly makes my office a more inviting place to be.

Ornamental Uses

Rosemary's needle-shaped green leaves are topped by lavender to purple flowers in summer, while some plants bloom pink. Varieties vary in their growth habits. Most are compact, upright plants that are just right for containers. Others cascade down stone walls, and one variety grows into a 6-foot-tall shrub. All rosemary plants need full sun and benefit from periodic trimming to keep them shapely. But beyond routine watering, feeding, and trimming, rosemary practically grows itself.

Growing Your Own Rosemary

Easily grown in any well-drained soil, rosemary's biggest limitation is its lack of winter hardiness. A few varieties such as 'Arp' rosemary can survive winters in Zones 6 to 7 (see "Know Your Hardiness Zone" on page 85), but most others die when exposed to temperatures below about 20°F. To complicate matters, plants are often so large by summer's end that bringing them indoors for the winter can be a problem. If your winters are too cold for rosemary, but you want to keep the same plant from year to year, root a few stem cuttings in late summer, pot these little plants, and keep them indoors through winter. Under good conditions, rosemary stems will strike roots in a month, and then be ready to transplant into their own pots a few weeks later. Set out young plants in mid spring, at about the time of your last frost. Water only during droughts, as rosemary prefers slightly dry conditions.

SAFFRON

USES:	culinary, ornamental
BOTANICAL NAME:	*Crocus sativus*
OTHER COMMON NAMES:	none
AREA OF ORIGIN:	Western Asia

Saffron is often considered the most expensive spice in the world. It is rare because it's made from the thin threadlike stigmas found in the open flowers of a little crocus that blooms only once a year in autumn. Each flower bears only three skinny threads, which must be harvested by hand. Only a small amount is needed to add distinctive flavor and yellow color to breads and rice or pasta dishes. Although many gardeners have great success growing saffron flowers, there is still a storage problem. Even under good conditions, dried saffron begins to lose its flavor after only four months.

These challenges are woven into the history of saffron, which goes back at least 4,000 years. In addition to its use as a spice, saffron has been used as a medicinal plant. Its active ingredient, crocetin, is a potent antioxidant that has been found to lower cholesterol in animal experiments and has inhibited growth of cancer cells in test-tube studies. Because of this, saffron may make its way into future medicines used to treat cancer, heart disease, and high blood pressure. However, saffron cures are not something to try at home—large amounts of pure saffron are poisonous. Saffron threads also have been used to

INEDIBLE LOOK-ALIKE
Another pretty bulb that produces lavender flowers in autumn, meadow saffron (*Colchicum autumnale*) is poisonous and should not be eaten. This plant grows from a bulb, not a corm, and its leaves are broader than those of true saffron.

make a bright orange dye, but historically, this dye is so precious, it has been reserved for dying the robes of monks and other important religious figures.

Culinary Uses

Saffron is most often paired with rice dishes like Spanish paella and Italian risotto, although it also may be used in breads, stews, cakes, and cheeses. Saffron's flavor is often described as a warm, piquant perfume, which seems more vibrant because of the rich yellow-orange color it brings to foods. To make the most of a pinch of dried saffron, soak it in a few teaspoons of water or stock for a few moments before adding it just as the dish approaches doneness. And only a pinch is needed. Using more in a recipe can lead to an unpleasantly bitter taste. When buying saffron, which is sold at most supermarkets and gourmet food stores, buy only a little at a time, and keep it in your freezer.

Ornamental Uses

Even if you never pick a thread, you may want to grow saffron for its flowers alone. Blooming in October, the little flowers are ideal for growing beneath a thin groundcover, such as creeping thyme, or they can be planted along the edge of your lawn. The leaves are grass-thin, and usually grow from autumn to spring, disappearing altogether in summer. The species blooms light lavender with darker purple veins in the petals and bright orange stamens in the center of each flower.

Growing Your Own Saffron

Saffron grows best in Zones 6 to 8 (see "Know Your Hardiness Zone" on page 85), in light-textured, well-drained soil in full sun. The plants are dormant from late spring to autumn, and corms (rounded, acorn-sized storage roots) may be planted anytime during this period. Mail-order suppliers normally ship them in early autumn. Plant the corms 3 inches deep and 6 inches apart. Sometimes saffron crocuses do not bloom until their second autumn after planting, but then they return for several seasons with little care. Dig, divide, and replant the corms about every five years. If your plants suddenly disappear, the problem is probably hungry mice, squirrels, or rabbits, all of which enjoy a breakfast of saffron corms on a cold winter day.

SAGE

USES:	medicinal, culinary, aromatic, ornamental
BOTANICAL NAME:	*Salvia officinalis*
OTHER COMMON NAMES:	garden sage
AREA OF ORIGIN:	Southern Europe

The classic flavoring herb for Thanksgiving stuffing, sage is also one of the most ancient of cultivated herbs. Associated with long life and good health, sage is renowned in the herbal traditions of Europe, China, and North America. In modern gardens, sage's gray-green leaves are among the most beautiful of all herbs, and a mature sage plant in full bloom is breathtaking to behold. The plant's short stems make great filler material for tussie-mussies and potpourri, or you can weave them into herbal wreaths.

Medicinal Uses

Sage has antibiotic properties, and sage tea is often recommended as a cure-all for the "I think I might be coming down with something" syndrome. Sage is also rich in vitamins A and C, and contains numerous antioxidant compounds. Sore throats, irritated gums, and mouth sores can be soothed by strong sage tea used as a gargle or mouthwash. Because of its potency, avoid using sage medicinally if you are pregnant or nursing.

Culinary Uses

The most common use for sage is as a seasoning for poultry or seafood stuffing, but a few pinches also work well with egg dishes. A few chopped fresh leaves can be a flavorful addition to cheese spreads as well. Use a light hand with this herb, because a little goes a long way. Gather leaves in early summer, just before the plants bloom, and dry them whole before storing in glass jars. (See page 45 for drying techniques.) Rub the dried leaves to crumble them just as you add them to cooked dishes.

Aromatic Uses

Sage is reputed to foster deep sleep, so it is often added to sweet pillows. The leaves are also attractive in potpourri. Short stems of sage make fine aromatic accents for herbal wreaths. Although the fresh leaves are flat, they curl as they dry.

Ornamental Uses

Positively luminous in the garden, sage looks good in the company of almost any other plant. Sage's lilac flowers, produced in midsummer, are beautiful as well. In addition to traditional garden sage with gray-green leaves, there are varieties blushed with purple, as well as variegated strains that are splashed with cream, purple, and green. Sage favors full sun in cool climates and can handle partial shade where summers are very hot.

Growing Your Own Sage

Hardy to Zone 4 (see "Know Your Hardiness Zone" on page 85), sage is best described as a short-lived perennial. Begin with small purchased plants in spring, which can be grown in beds or containers. Any well-drained soil with a slightly acidic pH is acceptable to sage. (See "Checking the Soil's pH" on page 88). During the first summer, pinch the stem tips back two or three times to encourage strong branching. Expect heavy blooming in the second year and into the third. After that, the plants usually become woody and ragged. To keep a strain indefinitely, root stem cuttings taken each summer, and set them out in autumn. Fertilize established plants in late spring as new growth appears, and then again in late summer.

NATIVE SAGES
North America is rich in native species of sage. Although not as tasty as European sage, they are very aromatic. Burning sage stems is an ancient Native American ritual.

ST. JOHN'S WORT

USES:	medicinal, ornamental
BOTANICAL NAME:	*Hypericum perforatum*
OTHER COMMON NAMES:	klammath weed
AREAS OF ORIGIN:	Europe, Western Asia

Treasured by herbalists and sorcerers for thousands of years, St. John's wort has been used to repel demons, heal wounds, and most recently, to cure the blues. It is also an interesting dye plant, producing a yellow to red pigment, depending on how it is handled in the cloth-dyeing process. This pretty yellow-flowered perennial gets its name from its tendency to bloom in Britain on St. John's Day, June 24. Easily grown in many climates and soils, St. John's wort is a common weed in many areas. To identify it in the wild, two field markings are useful. Upon finding a likely plant showing yellow five-petaled flowers with numerous stamens emerging from the centers, look for tiny black dots along the edges of the petals. Next, hold a leaf up to strong light and look for dark dots, which are oil glands. If these characteristics are present, you have stumbled upon a naturalized patch of St. John's wort.

Medicinal Uses

St. John's wort is the most widely used antidepressant medication in Europe, and numerous studies have shown that taking 900 milligrams daily of a standardized extract or tablet, usually split into three doses of 300 milligrams each, is a safe and effective treatment for mild to moderate depression. In addition to improving one's overall mood, after taking St. John's wort for several weeks, many people report sleeping better as well. And, unlike some prescription antidepressants, St. John's wort has very few side effects except for increased photosensitivity in susceptible individuals. Using sunscreen prevents this complication. If you have a ready supply of plants, you can easily make your own extract (see "Making Liquid Extracts" on page 32). One of the first things you will notice about this herb is that the flowers turn red when they are bruised. By the time an extract is complete, it is usually dark red in color.

If you are taking any prescription medications, consult your doctor before taking St. John's wort. Recent research has shown that this herb can cause many other drugs to become less effective, including some medications used to treat cancer, AIDS, high cholesterol, and irregular heartbeat. It may also reduce the effectiveness of some birth control pills.

Ornamental Uses

A cheery little perennial that grows less than 2 feet tall, St. John's wort spreads into a broad green mound topped by starry yellow flowers beginning in early summer. It is an excellent herb to grow along the edge of a walkway or lawn, or you can use it in a wildflower area interspersed with borage, chamomile, feverfew, and other herbs that reseed themselves with no help from humans.

Growing Your Own St. John's Wort

A tough perennial hardy to Zone 4 (see "Know Your Hardiness Zone" on page 85), St. John's wort will grow in full sun or partial shade. Any well-drained soil will suffice, evidenced by the fact that this herb often thrives on neglected roadsides. Seeds germinate sporadically, so it is usually best to begin with a purchased plant or a rooted cutting taken from a wild plant. St. John's wort is neither native nor endangered, so this is one herb you can dig from wild places with a clear conscience. In late summer, allow some of the flowers to mature and shed seeds in the garden. Individual plants often live only a few years, but they are easily succeeded by young offspring that pop up nearby. And, although St. John's wort is a willing grower, it is not usually an invasive plant.

To harvest St. John's wort for medicinal purposes or to make a rich yellow dye, cut off the top third of the plant and use the flowers along with the topmost leaves and stems. Within a few weeks, new flowers will appear. Opinions vary on the fragrance of St. John's wort plants. Some people wear gloves when cutting the tops because the sap's aroma is often reminiscent of turpentine.

SALAD BURNET

USES: culinary, ornamental

BOTANICAL NAME: *Poterium sanguisorba* (also known as *Sanguisorba minor*)

OTHER COMMON NAMES: burnet, pimpernel

AREAS OF ORIGIN: Europe, Western Asia

Salad burnet has been included in kitchen gardens for 2,000 years. Because its cucumber-flavored leaves must be used fresh, this herb is typically unknown to cooks who do not grow it themselves. Salad burnet is extremely easy to grow, and a single plant is enough to produce plenty of leaves, which can be added to salads and sandwiches or used as a colorful garnish. Although it was common for early Europeans to use this plant for a number of medicinal purposes, salad burnet's health benefits may be limited to the respectable amounts of vitamin C present in its lacy leaves.

Culinary Uses

The flavor of salad burnet's young fresh leaves is quite delicate. Simply pull individual leaves from the stems and toss them into salads, layer them in sandwiches, or chop them into cheese spreads (perhaps accompanied by dill, chervil, or chives). You can also use this herb's fresh leaves to garnish cold drinks or to decorate serving platters laden with chilled salad or fruit. Especially good when paired with cucumbers, salad burnet makes a fine substitute for fresh watercress in most recipes. "Fresh" is the only way to enjoy this herb, as its flavor is quickly lost when cooked, dried, or frozen.

Ornamental Uses

Salad burnet is a vibrantly attractive plant that grows into a fountain-shaped mound of long stems studded with dainty leaves with pink edges. In mid-summer, pink flower spikes form, raising the plant's height from 1 foot to nearly 3 feet. Salad burnet is often used as an edging plant, so any leaves caught underfoot will release their cucumber-fresh fragrance. Burnet's fresh blue-green leaf color contrasts well with herbs that have gray-green foliage, such as lavender or sage.

Growing Your Own Salad Burnet

A tough perennial hardy to Zone 4, this herb also can handle hot, humid summers in Zone 9 (see "Know Your Hardiness Zone" on page 85). You can start with seed or with a purchased plant set out in spring. Average garden soil, in a spot that gets at least a half day of sun, is fine for this herb. Salad burnet also can be grown in containers. Gather leaves as you need them in the kitchen. If the plants are allowed to flower and shed seed, expect to see volunteer plants scattered around your garden. Cutting back the flower spikes prevents seed formation and helps to force out a late summer crop of new leaves. Plants more than three years old may be dug up, the root mass cut into halves or quarters with a quick chop of a sharp knife or spade, and immediately replanted in early spring.

JEFFERSON'S GOURMET PASTURE

After noting the vigor of salad burnet in his own garden, Thomas Jefferson had it planted in a pasture where it provided food for livestock and helped control erosion.

SAVORY

USES: medicinal, culinary, ornamental

BOTANICAL NAME: *Satureja hortensis, S. montana*

OTHER COMMON NAMES: summer savory, winter savory

AREA OF ORIGIN: Mediterranean region

Two related herbs go under the name savory. Summer savory (*Satureja hortensis*) is a fine-flavored annual herb that goes with many foods, particularly vegetables and beans. Winter savory (*S. montana*) is a stiff little perennial that makes an attractive edging plant in the herb garden, but its strong, almost pine-like flavor makes it a challenge to use in the kitchen. Both types of savory have been popular in Europe for at least two centuries, primarily for flavoring foods but also for treating indigestion and regulating sex drive. Indeed, the botanical name is derived from satyr, a mythological half-man/half-goat woodland creature known for its sexual stamina. But like the satyrs themselves, savory's promise of promoting sexual vitality is more myth than fact.

Medicinal Uses

Summer savory contains several compounds with mild antiseptic properties, so you might sip a cup of savory tea to aid recovery from indigestion or diarrhea. Or use the tea as a gargle to soothe a minor sore throat.

Culinary Uses

Summer savory's flavor is reminiscent of both thyme and oregano, and can be substituted for these herbs in most recipes. Fresh or dried, use summer savory to season steamed or roasted vegetables from asparagus to summer squash, and include it in toppings for baked potatoes. It's also an excellent choice for seasoning breadcrumbs. Summer savory is often called "the bean herb" because its flavor works so well with beans, peas, and lentils. It also pairs well with fish. When dried and stored in a cool, dry place, summer savory keeps its flavor for many months. Buy whole leaves rather than the powdered form. If you dry your own savory, use the oven method, and try to keep the leaves whole as you pull them from the dried stems. (See page 46 for drying technique.) Crush the leaves just before adding them to foods.

Winter savory can be eaten, but it's important to use very small amounts of only the youngest, most tender leaves. Older leaves are peppery and have an almost pine-like scent, which is difficult to manage in the kitchen.

Ornamental Uses

Summer savory is a rather lax, rangy plant that tends to flop over in the garden, so it usually tastes better than it looks. The opposite is true of winter savory—a very neat, compact plant that grows into a tailored mound less than 1 foot tall. Use winter savory to edge herb beds, or put it to work as a foreground plant to hide the bare ankles of taller herbs such as lavender. Bees are attracted to winter savory's small white to lilac flowers that appear in midsummer. After flowering peaks, shear back the plants to keep them looking trim.

Growing Your Own Savory

Summer savory, an annual herb, benefits from a prompt start in spring. Either start fresh seed indoors a month before the last spring frost or buy seedlings in mid spring. Grow at least three plants to make sure you have plenty of stems for cutting and drying. Any fertile, well-drained soil with a near-neutral pH will do (see "Checking the Soil's pH" on page 88), or you can grow the plants in containers set in full sun. Begin cutting stems as you need them in the kitchen when the plants are 6 inches tall. At the first appearance of pale pink flowers at the stem tips, cut the stems for drying, leaving the bottom third of the plants intact. Provided with regular water, the plants will usually regrow a second crop of stems. Summer savory dies with the first hard frost of autumn.

Winter savory is hardy to Zone 6 (see "Know Your Hardiness Zone" on page 85), and its culture is very similar to that of other semi-woody Mediterranean herbs, such as lavender and oregano. Winter savory often retains a good supply of green leaves through winter. However, at winter's end, it is helpful to cut back the old stems to within 3 inches of the ground, which encourages the plants to develop vigorous new branches. Winter savory plants tend to be short-lived, often deteriorating after three years or so. Rooting stem cuttings taken in mid spring is always worth trying, or you can layer a stem or two each summer to make sure that you always have vigorous young plants coming along. (See "Propagating Perennial Herbs" on page 95.)

SCENTED GERANIUM

USES: aromatic, ornamental

BOTANICAL NAME: *Pelargonium* species and hybrids

OTHER COMMON NAMES: pelargonium, scented-leaf geranium

AREA OF ORIGIN: South Africa

Botanically speaking, scented geraniums are not geraniums at all, but then neither are the flowering "geraniums" that we so commonly see planted in beds and window boxes. Rather, all of these so-called geraniums are pelargoniums, tender perennials native to South Africa. True geraniums are mostly woodland wildflowers native to North America, but the geranium name has stuck with pelargoniums nonetheless.

Leaves of scented geraniums exhibit a delightful range of scents, including fruits (apple, lemon, and lime), spices (nutmeg and mint), flowers (rose and lemon-rose), and a catch-all category often called the pungents. Scented geraniums release their fragrances when the leaves are brushed or crushed. None can survive freezing roots, but any scented geranium can easily be grown as a winter houseplant that can be moved outdoors to a patio or porch in the summer. Container gardeners in particular enjoy assembling a small collection of these plants. The leaves of any variety can be dried for use in potpourri and sachets.

Aromatic Uses

Scented geraniums make vigorous growth in late spring, and leaves can be gathered at any time during the summer. It is customary to cut the plants back by half before bringing them indoors for the winter, which presents an excellent opportunity to collect leaves for drying. Dry them on a screen or in flat trays, or incorporate them into herbal wreaths made with fresh material. (See page 45 for drying techniques.)

Ornamental Uses

Scented geraniums do bloom, usually in early summer, but the flowers are small and not especially showy. And the size and texture of the foliage varies between varieties. For large, lush hanging baskets, either apple or nutmeg geraniums are top choices because of their almost vine-like growth habit. Rose geranium leaves are ferny in texture, and the large plants quickly fill a pot. Lemon geraniums are smaller plants, good for little containers. Specialty nurseries sell numerous other varieties, and hobbyists almost always propagate their plants from cuttings, often offering the rooted offspring for sale.

Growing Your Own Scented Geraniums

Adopt new plants in spring, potting them in any good light-textured potting soil. Place plants in a coolish spot where they will get a half day of sun. Water just before the soil becomes dry, and feed plants monthly with a mix-with-water fertilizer. In late summer or early autumn, shear plants back by half their size, gather the leaves for drying, and bring the plants indoors. Expect little growth during the winter, and water plants sparingly. Begin feeding them again in spring, and move them back outdoors after the last spring frost has passed. Hearty to Zones 8 and 9 (see "Know Your Hardiness Zone" on page 85), geraniums can be left outdoors in mild winter climates.

Scented geraniums are sold by both species and variety names. If you are a beginner, some tried-and-true varieties include 'Apple' (*Pelargonium odoratissimum*), 'Old Fashioned Rose' (*P. graveolens*), and 'Nutmeg' (*P. nervosum*). Nurseries sometimes give favorite varieties new names, resulting in a certain level of confusion. Several of the mail-order sources beginning on page 229 offer dozens of scented geraniums varieties.

SWEET WOODRUFF
USES: aromatic, ornamental
BOTANICAL NAME: *Galium odoratum*
OTHER COMMON NAMES: galium
AREAS OF ORIGIN: Europe, North Africa

This little herb is so beloved in Germany that its name there translates as "master of the woods." Most at home in the rich, moist soil of a shady forest floor, sweet woodruff makes a wonderful groundcover to grow beneath trees. And although this herb was long used for medicinal purposes, sweet woodruff contains coumarin, which has been linked to liver damage and may cause cancer. Rather than taking sweet woodruff internally, use the leaves in dried tussie-mussies, sachets, and potpourri. The fresh leaves have little fragrance, but after they have been dried, gently crushing them releases an aroma best described as vanilla mixed with newly mown hay.

Aromatic Uses

Sweet woodruff leaves must be dried before they attain a respectable level of fragrance. Gather the tallest stems, which are never more than 6 or 7 inches long, tie them together in small bunches and hang them to dry in a warm, airy place for about a week. (See page 45 for drying techniques.) Early summer is a good time to gather the leaves, and it does not matter whether or not the plants have yet produced their tiny white flowers. If you feel frustrated handling sweet woodruff's short stems, you can use scissors to gather stem tips by the handful. Dry the clipped stems on newspapers or screens.

Ornamental Uses

Sweet woodruff looks best in a shady area where it can spread into an informal drift, the same way it would in damp woods. It combines well with other woodland beauties, such as ferns, trilliums, hostas, and goldenseal. Sweet woodruff never grows taller than ankle-high, and although it does spread, it is easily pulled from places where it may not be wanted.

Growing Your Own Sweet Woodruff

Sweet woodruff seeds are slow and erratic germinators, so it's best to begin a planting with purchased plants, set out in early spring. A perennial hardy to Zone 4 (see "Know Your Hardiness Zone" on page 85), this herb likes very soft, moist soil that is rich in humus and has an acidic pH of around 5.5. (See "Checking the Soil's pH" on page 88.) So, add plenty of organic matter to the site, but not lime. Keep the new planting constantly moist through the first season. After that, plants should persist and spread for years with little care beyond occasional weeding and watering, and an annual springtime application of an all-purpose timed-release plant food. To propagate plants, dig up small rooted plantlets in early spring and transplant them immediately to where you want them to grow.

TANSY

USES: aromatic, ornamental

BOTANICAL NAME: *Tanacetum vulgare*

OTHER COMMON NAMES: none

AREA OF ORIGIN: Europe

The fact that tansy tea is one of the oldest known remedies for intestinal worms gives a clue as to why you should not put it in your mouth. It is poisonous. Although the potency of tansy plants varies among strains, all are potentially packed with the chemical compound thujone, which can cause convulsions or even death. It can do the same to garden insects, which is why many gardeners use tansy tea as a spray to repel pests from potatoes and cabbage. Tansy leaves that are strewn around places where ants enter buildings often deter them, and bunches of tansy flowers, hung in windows or doorways, reputedly discourage flies. The little yellow button-like flowers of tansy always make fine additions to herbal wreaths. And tansy's long, stout stems make its flowers popular in dried arrangements. In the garden, robust tansy plants are famous for getting carried away by their natural zest for life, so it's important to watch their spread.

Aromatic Uses

Tansy leaves give off a slightly camphor-like scent when brushed, which is not unpleasant in the garden. The fragrance of the leaves also discourages insects, and some gardeners rub the leaves on their clothes to deter buzzing gnats and flies. You also can make a tea from tansy leaves to use as an all-purpose garden insecticide. Adding a few drops of dishwashing liquid per quart of tansy tea will help the mixture stick to plant leaves.

Ornamental Uses

Tansy plants are quite tall, often growing to 4 feet or more, so it is a good plant for adding height at the back of the garden. Each plant produces several clusters of small rounded yellow flowers, borne on long stems that make them easy to harvest and dry in bunches. (See page 45 for drying techniques.) The finely cut, ferny leaves also make good filler material for fresh flower arrangements.

Growing Your Own Tansy

Tansy is a perennial, hardy to Zone 4 (see "Know Your Hardiness Zone" on page 85) and also very tolerant of hot, humid conditions. It grows almost too well and will become a weedy nuisance in the garden if it is not given regular discipline. The vigorous clumps become larger with each passing year. Always harvest the flowers to keep tansy from reseeding, and each spring use a sharp spade to cut around the clump and reduce its size.

Assuming you are willing to monitor tansy's exuberant growth, establish a new planting by setting out a purchased plant, seedling, or division taken from a clump in the early spring. Tansy likes full sun but is not picky about soil. Kept moist for a few weeks after planting, tansy needs no further care.

TANSY TOES
Hundreds of years ago, when people feared any illness that began with chills and fever, they stuffed tansy into shoes, believing it would prevent these symptoms.

Whenever you want a new plant, simply dig up a few stems, with the roots attached, from the outside of a clump and transplant the chunk to where you want more tansy.

TARRAGON'S FAMILY RELATIONS

In hot, humid climates where tarragon is difficult to grow, try Mexican tarragon, also known as sweet marigold. A tropical perennial grown as an annual, Mexican tarragon has leaves that taste similar to French tarragon. In Mexican cooking, they add flavor to tamales, stews, and even hot chocolate.

TARRAGON

USES: culinary

BOTANICAL NAME: *Artemisia dracunculus* var. *sativa*

OTHER COMMON NAMES: French tarragon

AREA OF ORIGIN: Central Russia

Sometime during the Middle Ages, a discriminating French cook noticed superior flavor in an unusual strain of "dragonwort"—the original common name for tarragon. It was probably so named because this plant with winding, serpentine roots was also used to treat snakebites. Unlike similar plants, this particular one in our unknown cook's kitchen had a clean anise-like flavor and no hint of earthy balsam. Knowing that he (or she) was on to something special, this long-forgotten cook began patiently propagating the plant, which stubbornly refused to bear fertile seed. In this way, the fine culinary herb known as French tarragon was born.

When you use French tarragon today, the herb in your hands is a direct descendent of the original, propagated and passed down from gardener to gardener for more than a thousand years. How can you tell if you have the real thing? If you bite into a leaf of fresh French tarragon, there will be a slight numbing sensation on the tongue, with flavor that is arrestingly anise-like with no trace of pine or leather. A closely related strain that can be grown from seed, Russian tarragon has flavor that is both weak and muddy at the same time.

Culinary Uses

Tarragon is teamed up with chervil, parsley, and chives in French *fines herbes*, in which the herbs are tied in bundles and used to flavor stocks, fish, and poultry. A light sprinkling of tarragon is also a fine way to add flavorful highlights to sauces such as buttery béarnaise, cream sauces, or sauces made with savory cheeses. Tarragon also fits in well with healthier updated sauces made with low-fat yogurt or reduced-fat sour cream. And it is perhaps the most popular herb for steeping in a good vinegar, which is then used to make salad dressings and tangy sauces for splashing onto salads or steamed vegetables.

In its dried form, tarragon is found on most supermarket spice shelves. Often, fresh versions are available, as well. Fresh is much better. If you have leftover stems, or if you grow your own tarragon, store any extra stems in the freezer in an airtight container. Frozen tarragon generally has better flavor than the dried version.

Growing Your Own Tarragon

A perennial hardy to Zone 4 (see "Know Your Hardiness Zone" on page 85), tarragon needs a certain combination of growing conditions to thrive. The soil should be fertile yet gritty and well drained, with a near neutral pH. (See "Checking the Soil's pH" on page 88.) Full sun to partial shade is ideal, or you can grow tarragon in pots. You must start with a purchased plant, because French tarragon is always propagated from stem cuttings or root division, and never from seed. Set out new plants in early spring, just before the last frost is expected. About six weeks after planting (or in mid spring for established plants) pinch back the growing tips to encourage branching. Pinch plants again in midsummer to force them to develop additional new growth.

Under warm, humid conditions, tarragon is subject to a number of diseases that cause its leaves to shrivel and die. To keep this from happening, keep the foliage as dry as possible. Avoid wetting the leaves when you water the plants, and mulch the root zone with 1 inch of sand or pebbles to help create a dry environment.

Over time, tarragon roots become so tangled that they tend to strangle themselves. Because of this, division is necessary maintenance. Dig up and divide plants every two to three years in early spring. Between divisions, you also can take stem cuttings in the spring and set them to root. Tarragon plants can be kept indoors through winter, though they require bright light to flourish. Outdoors, mulch over the plants after they become dormant in late autumn to protect them from winter injury.

THYME

USES:	medicinal, culinary, ornamental
BOTANICAL NAME:	*Thymus* species
OTHER COMMON NAMES:	English thyme, French thyme, mother of thyme
AREA OF ORIGIN:	Central Europe

Thyme pleases people in so many ways that it should be no surprise that there are more than 300 types currently in cultivation. The thymes used in cooking, broadly categorized as English or French, seem to go with almost everything, including salads, grains, vegetables, and meats. Then there are dainty lemon thymes, many of which feature scented variegated leaves. These are often the perfect choice when you want a little companion plant for container-grown flowers. A third group, the creeping thymes, may be employed as groundcovers, or planted between stones or in crevices, so that their fresh scent is released when trampled.

Medicinal Uses

Historically regarded as the herb of courage, thyme was once a leading medicinal herb for psychological problems, including shyness, nightmares, and melancholy moods. Thyme is a rich source of antioxidants, and its essential oil contains high concentrations of thymol, once used as a topical antibiotic. Too much is toxic, however, and thyme oil applied to the skin often causes serious irritation. Yet you are completely safe sipping a cup of thyme tea or using thyme liberally in cooking.

Culinary Uses

French and Creole cooking make heavy use of thyme, which has emerged as a favorite herb of innovative modern chefs. Simple dishes such as roasted vegetables are transformed into savory specialties and green salads reach new heights with the addition of thyme. Grain, pasta, or vegetable dishes that have cream sauce or cheese get a lift from thyme, and you can add it to dry rubs for meats. Thyme holds up well to long cooking times, and whenever fresh sprigs are available, they make a great final touch as an edible garnish. In addition to its flavor, perhaps another reason for thyme's popularity is that the dried leaves retain their culinary quality for a very long time. If you grow your own, you will be pleased to discover that the short stems studded with little leaves dry very quickly on screens or in a slow oven. When the leaves are crisp, strip them from the stems and store them whole in an airtight container.

Ornamental Uses

As container gardening and rock gardening have gained popularity, previously obscure types of thyme have emerged to fill the need for fine-textured, cascading plants with multiple talents. Although these designer thymes are not the top choices for culinary use, various lemon, golden, and variegated thymes are among the best plants you can grow in crevices, atop stone walls, or tucked inside the edge of a pot of pansies.

Growing Your Own Thyme

The first step in growing thyme is to choose the types you want to include in your garden. If your main interest is culinary, looks for thymes classified as *Thymus vulgaris,* including English thyme, which has deep green leaves. The leaves of French thyme (also *T. vulgaris*) are gray, with a mild, sweet flavor. Several creeping thymes with very small green leaves—for example lemon thyme (*T. x citriodorus*)—also are flavorful and well worth growing as culinary herbs. Taste them first, because many of the prettiest thymes such as silver-leafed 'Argenteus' and golden thyme, which has yellow variegated leaves, are lovely to look at but lack good flavor. However, they make wonderful additions to large containers planted with several different herbs.

There are also other species commonly called creeping thyme that are purely ornamental plants. These are usually classified as *T. praecox* (mother of thyme) or *T. pseudolanuginosus* (woolly thyme). These plants grow into blooming ground covers that are topped with rosy blossoms in early summer.

Regardless of species, all thymes share similar cultural requirements. Like their ancestors that grow wild on the dry mountains of Greece, all thymes need gritty, well-drained soil and plenty of fresh air and sunshine. At the same time, they benefit from regular feeding, which helps keep the plants lush and healthy. Set out purchased plants in spring, and expect to see new growth right away. If your objective is to gather lots of leaves to dry and use in cooking, make a major cutting in early summer as the plants gain height and prepare to flower. After being cut back by half their size, the plants will produce a replacement crop of flowering stems, which you can harvest in late summer. This is also the time to pot up varieties of thyme that may not be hardy in your area.

Although most thymes survive winter to Zone 4 or 5 (see "Know Your Hardiness Zone" on page 85), some of the prettier variegated types are more temperamental and are best brought indoors from late autumn to early spring.

Thyme plants often become woody and prone to disease by the time they are three years old. The best way to propagate most culinary thymes is to root stem cuttings taken in spring. Lemon thymes and creeping thymes can be dug up and divided, preferably in early spring, just as new growth begins.

VALERIAN

USES: medicinal, aromatic, ornamental

BOTANICAL NAME: *Valeriana officinalis*

OTHER COMMON NAMES: none

AREAS OF ORIGIN: Europe, Asia

Valerian is best known as the sleep herb, and numerous studies have validated that it works. In times past, valerian was also used to season meat and to perfume soap, which is hard to believe considering the aroma of valerian root resembles that of dirty socks. The smell is attractive to cats, and valerian is sometimes added to catnip toys to make them even more attractive to felines.

Medicinal Uses

With valerian, the plant part used medicinally is the root, which contains compounds known as valepotriates. These are the active ingredients that reduce anxiety and promote restful sleep. You can take valerian as a tea or liquid extract, but the problem is with the flavor. Valerian tastes bad. Because of this, many people prefer capsules, which have the added benefit of providing standardized dosing. With valerian, it is important to buy products that provide standardized or guaranteed content. Accept no substitutions. Also note that valerian is most effective when it is taken daily, so don't expect results after taking it once. Most people begin sleeping better after their third or fourth day on valerian. The typical dose is a capsule or tablet providing a standardized dose of 300 to 600 milligrams of valerenic acid one hour before bedtime. Most studies are based on 600-milligram dosing. Side effects are rare, and most people who take valerian are pleased with how alert they feel upon awakening in the morning. Problems with drug interactions have not been reported with valerian, and its safety record is extremely strong. The few case reports of trouble with valerian are believed to have been the result of taking very high doses several times a day.

Aromatic Uses

If you want to please a cat, slip some dried valerian leaves or dried root into a cat toy. In gardens, cats sometimes discover plants and enjoy rubbing or rolling on them. You can also use valerian essential oil (sold at health food stores) to attract your cat to a scratching post or special sleeping place.

Ornamental Uses

Valerian is an old garden favorite, although by modern standards, the plants are somewhat rough and rangy. Growing to 5 feet tall in partial shade, this is a good plant for the rear of the herb garden. Clusters of pink flowers appear atop plants in early summer.

Growing Your Own Valerian

A vigorous perennial hardy to Zone 4 (see "Know Your Hardiness Zone" on page 85), valerian is best established from a purchased plant, because the seeds are poor germinators. Valerian likes rich, moist garden soil amended with composted manure or a timed-release plant food. Plants reach their full size in their second year. After that, dig up and divide clumps every three to four years to relieve overcrowding. Propagate plants by planting divisions dug from the mother clump. The best time to harvest roots for medicinal purposes is in autumn, as soon as the plants begin dying back. Scrub the roots well, and then cut them into thin slices and dry until crisp. Place in glass jars or another airtight container and store in a dark, cool place. Most gardeners who preserve valerian for medicinal purposes use fresh or dried roots to make a liquid extract (see "Making Liquid Extracts" on page 32).

YARROW

USES: medicinal, ornamental

BOTANICAL NAME: *Achillea millefolium*

OTHER COMMON NAMES: milfoil

AREA OF ORIGIN: Europe

Yarrow has shared the close company of humankind for tens of thousands of years, serving as medicine, a fortune-telling charm, and today, as a sturdy garden flower. Yarrow pollen has been found in burial caves dating back 60,000 years, and legend tells how Achilles used it during the Trojan War to stop the bleeding of battlefield wounds. Yarrow also found widespread use among Native American tribes, who used closely related native species to treat numerous illnesses and injuries. Historically, yarrow was a rather lackluster little flower best known for its ferny leaves, but in the last few decades, that has changed. Plant breeders have brought exciting color to the species, which now blooms in many shades of pink, yellow, red, and white. Yarrow is a fresh flower arranger's dream, and the blossom clusters make lasting dried flowers, too.

Medicinal Uses

Yarrow has a complex chemistry, which is probably why it has been used to treat so many different ailments. Scientists are still studying the active compounds in lesser-known yarrow cousins, but little research has been done on the practical use of yarrow by human beings. However, two medicinal uses have persisted through the ages, and are still widely recommended by herbalists. One is to use yarrow tea (made by steeping 2 teaspoons of dried yarrow leaves in a cup for water for ten minutes) to intensify fevers that mark the onset of a cold or flu. Taken a half cup at a time for a period of four hours, yarrow tea is thought to raise the fever slightly, thereby supporting the body's reaction to the pathogen—a process that is already underway. However, because yarrow tea contains at least two potentially toxic substances—coumarin and thujone—it should be taken only occasionally and always in moderation.

YARROW IN LOVE
If you're waiting for love to find you, placing yarrow under your pillow is supposed to foster dreams in which you will see your love to be.

You can also use yarrow leaves, fresh or dried, to make a poultice to help heal bruises or reduce swelling. Some people develop contact dermatitis from yarrow, but this reaction usually passes quickly.

If you want to gather your own yarrow to use medicinally, pick individual perfect leaves in early summer before the plants flower, and dry them on a screen or newspapers before storing them in an airtight container.

Ornamental Uses

Yarrow provides soft texture and warm color in any sunny flowerbed, and it is extremely easy to grow. Numerous varieties have been developed in recent years that have greatly improved the color range of this species. An award-winning mixture called 'Summer Pastels' blooms in a rainbow of soft colors, including yellow, pink, and purple. Other strains such as 'Cerise Queen' bloom red. A closely related species with a taller, more upright growth habit, yellow yarrow (*A. filipendulina*) is often used to separate rowdier colors in the garden. To dry any type of yarrow flower, gather the stems as soon as the flowers are fully open, bind them into small bunches with rubber bands, and hang them to dry in a warm, well-ventilated place.

Growing Your Own Yarrow

Hardy to Zone 2 (see "Know Your Hardiness Zone" on page 85), yarrow is a very resilient perennial that asks only for good sun, fertile and fast-draining soil, and spring rainfall. Many strains can be started from seed, but you will gain a full season's growth by setting out purchased plants in early spring. Place plants at least 12 inches apart. In their second season, they will grow together to form a mound of gray-green foliage topped by flattened clusters of flowers. Remove the spent flowers when they turn brown to help keep the planting looking neat.

Dig, divide, and replant established yarrow every three to four years to help keep the plants vigorous and healthy. Between replantings, you can propagate yarrow by cutting out rooted crowns that are close to the mother plant with a sharp knife, and replanting them immediately where you want them to grow.

Conclusion

 Wonderful things happen when you let herbs into your life. Whether you are plucking leaves from a sprig of thyme to toss into your pasta, soothing a sore throat with a warm cup of echinacea tea, or tucking lavender sachets into your linen closet, you'll see how herbs simply make life better. It's something you will learn each time you work—or play—with herbs.

I hope that this book will help you use herbs with confidence. The information here should take much of the mystery out of medicinal herbs, so that they become trusted allies in your quest for optimum health. Using culinary herbs will surely make you a more creative cook, and the timeless allure of fragrant herbs may win them a place in every room of your house. You will probably become so devoted to a few favorite herbs that you will want to grow them yourself. As garden plants, herbs have stood a test of time that has spanned many centuries.

With the help of this book, I hope you will welcome all of the riches that herbs can bring into your life. The more you use these gifts of the earth, the more you will wonder how you ever got along without them. It cannot be denied that Nature wants us to know, value, and use the treasured plants we call herbs.

Resources

Seeds, Plants, and Supplies

It is well worth the trouble to seek out a good source of herb plants close to home. If you cannot find locally grown herbs, or if you simply want access to a broader selection, the nurseries and seed merchants included here should help. I have selected nearly two dozen companies located in different parts of the United States and Canada, all of which sell at least some of their products on the Internet and/or through a mail-order catalog. Many also operate retail shops.

Companion Plants
7247 N. Coolville Ridge Road
Athens, OH 45701
740-592-4643
www.companionplants.com
Offers hundreds of varieties of herb plants and seeds, including all of the best lavenders.

Dabney Herbs
P.O. Box 22061
Louisville, KY 40252
502-893-5198
www.dabneyherbs.com
Sells a bonanza of artemisias, scented geraniums, and many other herb plants, plus essential oils.

Garden Medicinals and Culinaries
P.O. Box 320
Earlysville, VA 22936
434-964-9113
www.gardenmedicinals.com
*All of the growable medicinal herbs are here along with
eighteen basils and lots of other culinaries. Also sells
bottles for extracts and other herb-handling supplies.*

Greenfield Herb Garden
310 Harrison Street
P.O. Box 9
Shipshewana, IN 46565
800-831-0504
www.herb-garden.com
*Offers a very extensive selection of herb seeds and
supplies, which are sold by mail and online. Plants
must be purchased at the retail shop, but the selection
is so impressive that it's worth the trip.*

Heirloom Seeds
P.O. Box 245
W. Elizabeth, PA 15088
412-384-0852
www.heirloomseeds.com
Sells medicinal, culinary, and aromatic herb seeds.

In Harmony Herbs and Spices
P.O. Box 7555
4808 Santa Monica Avenue
San Diego, CA 92107
619-223-8051; 800-514-3727
www.inharmonyherbs.com
*Has thousands of different bulk dried herbs, herb seeds,
herb crafting supplies, and aromatherapy products.
Retail store in San Diego.*

Johnny's Selected Seeds
1 Foss Hill Road
Albion, ME 04910
207-437-4301
www.johnnyseeds.com
*This extremely reputable company sells a fine selection
of herb seeds, including more than a dozen basils,
several calendulas, and five species of echinacea.*

Misty Ridge Herb Farm
P.O. Box 126
7350 W 14 Rd
Mesick, MI 49668
231-885-2290
www.herbplantsonline.com
*Herb plants are grown to order, then shipped late
spring. Good selection of proven varieties.*

Mountain Rose Herbs
85472 Dilley Lane
Eugene, OR 97405
800-879-3337
www.mountainroseherbs.com
*Has good selection of medicinal and culinary herb seeds,
capsules, liquid extracts, and essential oils.*

Nichols Garden Nursery
1190 Old Salem Road NE
Albany, OR 97321
800-422-3985
www.nicholsgardennursery.com
*Offers large selection of herb seeds, herb plants (shipped
in spring), and hops rooted cuttings, along with supplies
for herbal crafts. Retail shop in Albany, Oregon.*

Papa Geno's Herb Farm

11125 South 14th Street
Roca, NE 68430
402-423-5051
www.papagenos.com

This company's vast selection of herb plants includes 125 scented geraniums.

Pinetree Garden Seeds

P.O. Box 300
New Gloucester, ME 04260
207-926-3400
www.superseeds.com

Stocks a great selection of herb seeds in little packets, ideal for the small-scale gardener.

Possum Creek Herb Farm

528 Nature Trail
Soddy Daisy, TN 37379
423-332-0347
www.possumcreekherb.com

Family-run herb farm sells herb plants of all types and is open for visitors from spring to autumn.

Renee's Garden

888-880-7228 (to locate retailer nearby)
831-335-7228 (for gardening information)
www.reneesgarden.com

Has excellent selection of culinary and ornamental herb seeds sold primarily at garden centers and herb shops, but also through its website.

Richters

Goodwood, Ontario
L0C 1A0 Canada
905-640-6677
www.richters.com

Sells more than 900 varieties of all types of herbs, many available as both seeds and plants.

Sandy Mush Herb Nursery

316 Surrett Cove Rd.
Leicester, NC 28748
828-683-2014
www.brwm.org/sandymushherbs

Get the printed catalog from this venerable herb company, which sells plants of many rare herbs, or call ahead to visit Thursday through Saturday in season.

Seeds for the South

410 Whaley Pond Road
Graniteville, SC 29829
www.vegetableseedwarehouse.com

Offers culinary herb seeds selected for warm climates, including numerous types of basil.

Seeds of Change

P.O. Box 15700
Santa Fe, NM 87506
888-762-7333
www.seedsofchange.com

Sells organically grown seeds of most major culinary and medicinal herbs.

Sunnyboy Gardens, Inc.
3314 Earlysville Road
Earlysville, VA 22936
888-431-0006
www.sunnyboygardens.com

Has extensive selection of herb plants, including the most fragrant lavenders and hardiest rosemaries.

The Herb Cottage
442 CR 233
Hallettsville, TX 77964
979-562-2153
www.theherbcottage.com

Midway between Houston and San Antonio, this herb farm sells plants, retail and online, in autumn as well as spring (when Texas gardeners need them).

The Thyme Garden Herb Company
20546 Alsea Highway
Alsea, OR 97324
541-487-8671
www.thymegarden.com

Offers incredible selection of seeds, supplies, and herbs, including vegetatively propagated varieties of thyme, rosemary, hops, and hard-to-find lavenders.

Well-Sweep Herb Farm
205 Mount Bethel Road
Port Murray, NJ 07865
908-852-5390
www.wellsweep.com

Has huge selection of all types of herb plants available by mail. You can also visit the farm to see thousands of varieties as they grow in a garden.

Weslyn Farm
P.O. Box 21
Jobstown, NJ 08041
609-723-2115
www.weslynfarm.com

Sells herb plants and seeds, available retail or online, including an excellent selection of scented geraniums and a range of vegetatively cultivated sages.

Organizations

The following organizations can supply helpful information on herbs and natural medicine, and answer any questions you may have. Some also provide referrals for herbalists in your area. Other ways to locate practitioners of herbal medicine is by looking in the yellow pages under (or doing an online search for) "herbalists," "naturopaths," "holistic practitioners," and/or "health services."

American Association of Naturopathic Physicians (AANP)
3201 New Mexico Avenue NW, Suite 350
Washington, DC 20016
866-538-2267; Fax: 202-274-1992
www.naturopathic.org

American Botanical Council (ABC)
6200 Manor Road
Austin, TX 78723
512-926-4900; Fax: 512-926-2345
E-mail: abc@herbalgram.org
www.herbalgram.org

American Holistic Medical Association (AHMA)
12101 Menaul Boulevard NE, Suite C
Albuquerque, NM 87112
505-292-7788; Fax: 505-293-7582
E-mail: info@holisticmedicine.org
www.holisticmedicine.org

Herb Research Foundation (HRF)
4140 15th Street
Boulder, CO 80304
303-449-2265; Fax: 303-449-7849
E-mail: info@herbs.org
www.herbs.org

Index

YOUR GUIDE TO ALTERNATIVE MEDICINE

Understanding, Locating, and Selecting Holistic Treatments and Practitioners

Larry P. Credit, Sharon G. Hartunian, and Margaret J. Nowak

The growing world of complementary medicine offers safe and effective solutions to many health disorders, from backache to headache. You may already be interested in alternative care approaches, but if you're like most people, you have a hundred and one questions you'd like answered before you choose a treatment. "Will I feel the acupuncture needles?" "What is a homeopathic remedy?" "Does chiropractic hurt?" *Your Guide to Alternative Medicine* provides the fundamental facts necessary to choose an effective complementary care therapy and begin treatment.

This comprehensive reference clearly explains numerous approaches in an easy-to-read format. For every complementary care option discussed, there is a description and brief history; a list of conditions that respond; information on the cost and duration of treatment; credentials and educational background for practitioners; and more. To find those therapies most appropriate for a specific condition, there is even a unique troubleshooting chart.

Your Guide to Alternative Medicine introduces you to options that you may never have considered—techniques that enhance the body's natural healing potential and have few, if any, side effects. Here is a reference that can help you make informed decisions about all your important healthcare needs.

$11.95 • 208 pages • 6 x 9-inch quality paperback • Health/Alternative Therapies/Reference • ISBN 0-7570-0125-4

GOING WILD IN THE KITCHEN
The Fresh & Sassy Tastes of Vegetarian Cooking
Leslie Cerier

Going Wild in the Kitchen is the first comprehensive global vegetarian cookbook to go beyond the standard organic beans, vegetables, and grains. In addition to providing helpful cooking tips, the book contains over 200 kitchen-tested recipes for healthful, taste-tempting dishes that call for such unique ingredients as edible flowers; sea vegetables; and wild mushrooms, berries, and herbs. It encourages the creative side of novice and seasoned cooks alike, prompting them to "go wild" in the kitchen by adding, changing, or substituting ingredients in existing recipes. Beautiful color photographs and a helpful resource list for finding organic foods complete this user-friendly cookbook.

$16.95 • 224 pages • 7.5 x 9-inch quality paperback • 2-Color • Full-color photos • Cooking/Vegetarian • ISBN 0-7570-0091-6

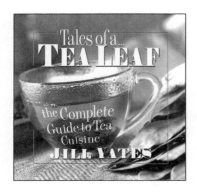

TALES OF A TEA LEAF
The Complete Guide to Tea Cuisine
Jill Yates

For devoted tea drinkers everywhere, *Tales of a Tea Leaf*—a complete guide to the intricacies of tea lore, tea brewing, and tea cuisine—is here. The book begins with an exploration of the legends and lore of tea, including its mysterious age-old relationship with rebels and smugglers. It presents the many tea types and brewing methods, as well as the miraculous health benefits of the tea leaf. What follows next is a collection of delicious tea beverages, from refreshing iced drinks to warm, spicy brews, as well as other wonderful creations, such as Apricot Tea Bread and Pumpkin Chai Pie. One thing is certain—you don't need to be a tea lover to enjoy *Tales of a Tea Leaf.*

$13.95 • 208 pages • 7.5 x 7.5-inch quality paperback • 2-Color • Cooking/Beverages/Tea • ISBN 0-7570-0099-1

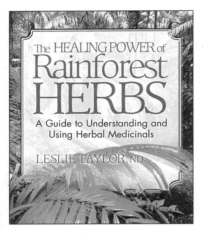

THE HEALING POWER OF RAINFOREST HERBS
A Guide to Understanding and Using Herbal Medicinals
Leslie Taylor, ND

Rainforests contain an amazing abundance of plant life—just two-and-a-half acres of Amazon rainforest are believed to house approximately 900 tons of botanicals. Even more exciting is the fact that scientists and researchers have only just begun to uncover the medicinal properties of rainforest herbs and flora. Nature has provided us with a treasure of herbal remedies— secrets that offer new approaches to health and healing. *The Healing Power of Rainforest Herbs* is a valuable guide to these herbs and their uses.

Detailing more than fifty rainforest botanicals, *The Healing Power of Rainforest Herbs* is the result of years of extensive research by naturopath Leslie Taylor. In it, she explains the medicinal properties of each herb and the natural chemicals involved, as well as preparation instructions. The author has also included the history of the herbs' use by indigenous peoples, and their current usage by natural health practitioners around the world. Helpful tables provide a quick guide to choosing the most useful botanicals for specific ailments. Illustrations of plants and recipes for herbal remedies complete the wealth of information found in this resource.

The Healing Power of Rainforest Herbs offers a blend of ancient and modern knowledge in an accessible reference guide. This unique book incorporates the healing practices of shamans with scientific research for anyone seeking to discover the medicinal secrets of the rainforest.

$18.95 • 268 pages • 7.5 x 9-inch quality paperback • 2-Color • Health/Herbs • ISBN 0-7570-0144-0